Pushing Through
It's YOUR Attitude

Paul Fowler

Copyright © 2020 Paul Fowler

All rights reserved. This book or any portion thereof may not be reproduced or used in any manner whatsoever without the express written permission of the publisher

Cover Photo by Jan Fowler

Cover Design by Paul Fowler

First Printing

ISBN: 978-1-7345261-2-7 ISBN

DEDICATION

To my friend Larry Hawkes who "called" me to be a Scoutmaster and my friend DJ Bott who encouraged it... and to my dear wife who had to endure it.

CONTENTS

	Acknowledgments	i
	Introduction	iii
1	Do Over	1
2	The Test	9
3	Are There Yet?	17
4	Build It. They Will Come	25
5	Camp Fowler	29
6	Bad Water	35
7	White Rock	41
8	Giving Your Best	45
9	Breakfast in The Bag	49
10	Winter Camp	57
11	Surviving Canada	63
12	Put the Bar Back	79
13	The Word Service	81
14	What People Miss	87
15	Things I wish Parents Understood	91
16	Conclusion	95
	Appendix	99

ACKNOWLEDGMENTS

Thank you, Mike Perkins, for the encouragement. Thank you, Casey Hall, Glen Curtis and Dale Cottrell, for proof reading.
Scouts, it's just around a corner and few hundred yards more. Thanks, for the memories.

Introduction

I hope that you find some humor and some inspiration in the stories I've included. I lay no claim to be a writer, so I hope you are not reading this to be impressed with my skills in the craft of writing. I am simply sharing stories of real experiences in hopes that some of you may be inspired to work with our youth in various organizations, religions, and clubs. For others, my hope is that you will do better than you are. May we appreciate our responsibility and our opportunity to shape the future by lifting and influencing the rising generation. Our world needs leaders of sound character. They need you and I to step up.

This book exposes my own weaknesses and the growth that took place within myself on this journey of working with our youth. Because of this, there may be a few pokes to some parents and others who, I feel, could do a better job.

We are indeed failing our sons by continuously lowering the bar of expectation by not teaching them *masculinity*, to have a *work ethic* – the ability to get up and get stuff done. We need to teach *citizenry* and the meaning of *patriotism*. These things are good for the whole of society and they make us all stronger.

We are protecting our sons too much. We as parents and leaders keep them from reaching their full potential. We need to teach them that it is okay to fail, if you get back up. Oh, and it is okay to get dirty, sometimes. And when they get hurt, we need to teach them to dust themselves off and go at it again. Teach them to be men. Teach them that life will bump them around sometimes and that is okay too. Life will not always be easy. Life can be great, but that is ultimately up to YOU.

I was in a leadership training session a few years back. The presenter, Elder Bruce D. Porter, said, "The problem we have regarding our youth isn't that we aren't hitting the target. It's that <u>we are aiming too low and *hitting* the target!</u>"

Our young men will almost always rise to the level of what is expected of them. We as leaders and them as youth <u>can do far more than we know</u>. We must learn to expect it.

So, go, teach them, inspire them, and set the bar up high for them to see.

Paul Fowler (PTFSM)

1 DO OVER

Cael is an Eagle Scout now. I often recall with fondness the first visits that he made to our troop. My wife and I were new as 11-year-old leaders in our congregation. For those who are not members of the Church of Jesus Christ of Latter Days Saints, we were assigned as leaders of First-year Scouts.

Cael, with all the excitement and energy an eleven-year-old could have, arrived at one of the meetings with a machete swinging through the closed quartered meeting room. With his big eyes wide open, and using all the enthusiasm of his youth, asked "Hey is it okay if I have this here?" I hesitantly answered sure, as long as it was strapped down to his leg. This was a tall order, since the machete appeared to be longer than his leg.

And so, I began my fourth assignment as a Scout leader. I was eager to get going, a huge improvement and contrast when compared to my first assignment.

Looking back at my first time being assigned, I admittedly had no clue what Scouting really was, what a leader was supposed to do, and even less what the Scouts needed to be doing. I was a lousy leader. I had been assigned to the position and told to show up on Tuesdays at our church and "take care of the boys." I did just that. I showed up on Tuesdays and listened to another 'Scout leader' read sections of the Scout Manual to the boys who, often, were climbing the walls. I saw little point in this activity or any benefit to the boys. In time, the other leader was 'released', and I was left alone to 'entertain' them.

My work of the time was in the copier field. I did what I knew. I brought defunct copiers to the Scouts on gurneys, like dead bodies, and the boys and I dissected them. They explored the units as if they were some form of erector set. Together, we experimented with the mirrors, lenses and servos that made up the guts of the machines. I am sure that their mothers were thrilled when I sent various parts home with the Scouts.

I was accomplishing my 'assignment' of entertaining the boys but failing in all things 'Scouting'. I had been left to my own devices without any training or guidance while serving in this capacity. I was not working to make a difference in their lives, instead I was simply passing the time. I was clueless. This was the first time in my adult life working with youth. I doubt that these boys were left with anything remarkable about having spent this time, their first year in Scouts with me. Either way, after about a year, my first stint as an 11-year-old leader ended.

My second opportunity came and went without much effort or improvement on my part. I was an advisor for Varsity-aged Scouts. I would love to mention all the things that I learned, but at the time, my own attitude stood in the way of any progress that I may have otherwise made. I simply dutifully marked time.

As I write this book, much of what I say regarding Scouting, has come to me as knowledge and experience after having served in numerous positions, and several troops. It took three opportunities before I could begin to see the bigger picture and enthusiastically engage myself. Now, I can reflect with gratitude at the wisdom that I have gained from these opportunities.

Much of what I have to say applies to our youth, boys and girls across the various organizations.

One of the tragedies regarding our youth is that we propagate bad experiences through our lack of training and knowledge. We lack empathy. Some of us won't make the effort to truly influence these youth. Others of us had poorly trained or motivated leaders from our youth and we, at times, pass the same behaviors on. We lack the vision of the why we do Scouting. We've been voluntold or have been assigned and sadly lack the passion and energy required to become immersed in the life work of building the youth in our communities. I include myself in the list of those who were not well trained, at least in the beginning.

We need to always have a purpose and direction when working with youth. We, as leaders, should be strengthening their families and strengthening the youth, not merely entertaining them.

The responsibility of leading or mentoring can be overwhelming. As a leader, the first place to start is to make sure that we, ourselves, are of a sound character and a good example as youth will learn the most from seeing what we do. They will imitate us. Next is to start learning, training, and seeking out a strong mentor, someone who has worked with youth in the past, someone who you can share experiences with and point you in the right direction at times. It also helps to have some encouragement from time to time. Things will not always go as planned.

What happened next to me was unforeseen and yet a great benefit. You too will find that as you seek help, knowledge, and skills to improve your leadership abilities, you will have unwittingly embarked on a path to self-improvement.

My third opportunity was the one that eventually took hold of my soul. It was the first time I was "called" (aka voluntold) as a Scoutmaster. I was reluctant to accept the assignment and refused to do it, at first. It required some time and a good talk with God before I could come around to committing myself to the position. At that time, I had a very poor perception of Scouting. I was less than impressed with my own first go around as the 11-Year-Old Scout leader. My first experience was a waste of my time and theirs. I was not impressed with what I observed Scouting to be. It appeared to be some middle-aged man without any apparent purpose, attempting to babysit and entertain the neighborhood kids. It was being used, in my exposure to "keep people busy". I had too many obligations to have an interest in being a part of that.

The Scouting that I remember from my youth, was both challenging and dynamic. It was moving and doing. The experiences truly had impact on me and have influenced my life.

Time would also be a challenge for me, as I owned and participated in multiple companies requiring the bulk of my time. What little time I had away from work, I spent with my own family. We camped 8 or 9 times a year as a family and extended family. By camping, I am mostly referring to taking our 42' land yacht and 4-wheelers to go boondocking. All the amenities of living at home were included. I suppose, in a very real sense, it wasn't really camping so much as living in our second home. We had movies with a big screen, microwave, refrigerator, beds, showers... well, you get the idea.

Though they promised me it wouldn't be so, asking me to be a Scoutmaster was asking me to give this all up and to spend time with someone else's boys. Over time, it would mean doing as the Scouts do. It would come to mean sleeping in hot, sweaty tents instead of air-conditioned rooms, hiking for miles in lieu of sightseeing from a 4-

wheeler and giving up my day off to do service. Eating something burnt over a fire with ash and dirt mixed in it, would replace my usual home cooked meals. My Saturday BBQs would now become neighborhood food-drives. All my vacation time would now be spent camping with the boys at summer camp.

Did I mention winter camping? That's what they call it when you willingly leaving a warm bed to sleep in a pile of snow in the sub-zero weather. It is so named because if we called it what it truly is, no one would go.

The time commitment that they tell you in the beginning is either a myth, propagated by the ignorant, or an outright lie to get you going. "Take your trailer," they said. "Take your dog," they said. "Give up 4-wheeling? Nay," they said. "It will be fun," they said. At least they got the last one correct.

In time, I came to understand that no Scoutmaster worth his salt could ever spend an hour or two per week and even come close to getting the job done. To truly become an effective leader of youth, you must become involved in their life to some degree. Knowing their concerns and needs will help you to connect with them. What other interest do they have? Do they have stresses or anxieties about life? What motivates them? What is their home life like?

Before going further, I want to say that working with the youth has been one of the best decisions I've made. Scouting has changed the trajectory of my own life in the same way it has millions of others. I'm grateful for having had the opportunity. It has improved the outlook of my own life, and those near to me, immeasurably.

It took a few days, several conversations with friends and with those who were attempting to talk me into this new "assignment", together with some real soul-searching to accept this new role. I decided that if I were to do this, I could not do it halfway. I did not want to be that guy who was just keeping kids busy. I jumped in headfirst, because it was "All in or not at all", as I would later teach the Scouts. And I became fully immersed in Scouting.

On my way to becoming fully immersed or pickled in Scouting, I actively sought out knowledge, training, equipment, and associations that would help me be an influencer. If I were to be involved, I wanted to have a true purpose. If I were going to invest myself and resources, I wanted to make a difference. In time, I came to understand how to work with the youth and, of course, to learn what Scouting was about. I wanted to "do my best".

In my research and zest for knowledge, I came across a copy of

Baden Powell's Scoutmaster handbook from 1932 and studied it. I found the original Scouting requirements to be much stricter and more challenging. This motivated me more than you will ever know. *True Scouting, it seemed, was more about the experiences and less about the check list.* Advancement was meant to be a natural byproduct of participation and not the focal point of what we do. I found this information refreshing and a stark contrast to what I had been observing. Our current culture did not seem to care about the experiences so much as the checklist.

A vision of what Scouting was meant to be was forming in my mind. It was, by design, meant to give the boys experiences and privations. It was learning by doing. It was helping them to connect with Heaven. It was leadership and character development. It tested them. Through participation, it built their self-esteem in a very authentic, organic and self-sufficient way. There is so much more here than just another activity or sport. Scouting done right was powerful and dynamic. This new view was fueling my passion for working with the boys.

To add more to the lure of the past, we visited the Norman Rockwell Art Exhibit as a troop. After viewing Scouting through his eyes, my mind was even more tainted with visions of how things were and could be in working with these Scouts. I was now forming a vison of and seeing Scouting for the first time in my adult life.

Though I cannot recall the reference, I once read the Scoutmaster's oath.

"Never do for a boy, what he can do for himself"

This hit me, as great advice for us all, leaders, Scoutmasters, teachers, and even parents. Our sons would all be much better off, even more manly and mature, if we applied this advice to our interactions with them.

I knew the youth in Troop #210 from my previous leadership position in our church congregation. I geared up and grabbed a new attitude. Armed with this new enlightenment and high expectations, I went on the first campout as Scoutmaster of Troop #210. This is where the expectations of the previous troop culture began to crash with true Scouting Ideals or at least with my Norman Rockwell view of how it should be. Some of our adventures as Troop #210, unfold in the following chapters.

WHEN FISHING YOU DON'T BAIT THE HOOK WITH FOOD YOU LIKE.

You bait the hook with food that the fish likes.

Working with youth is the same.

2 THE TEST

It was springtime. We arrived at our destination in Left Hand Fork, in a beautiful canyon with an ice-cold river running alongside the campsite, just outside of Hyrum, Utah. This would be my first camp with Troop #210. It was a safe place to go as I had frequented this location over the years with my family and I knew its layout beforehand. The availability of parking next to the campsite would reduce the stress of locating and setting up our site.

Soon after arriving, we began to set up camp. We selected the spot for the campfire, and we were laying out the locations for tents. It was then that we discovered that we had the wrong poles for the Springbar Tent. It is also possible that we had no clue how to use them.

After looking around to see what we had to use in our bin of possibilities, we settled on using electrician's tape. Using the tape, we converted the poles that we had into something that would hold the tent up. "Hey, can I put my tent here?" one Scout yelled out. He was indicating a spot so close to the fire pit, that he would be able to roast marshmallows from his bed.

"Not a good idea," I responded.

"Hey, Scoutmaster, where is your camp chef?" said another.

"I didn't bring one," I replied.

"How are we going to cook our food?" they asked.

"On a campfire," I answered.

"Hey who is going to set up my tent?"

"You are," I responded.

This is where the contest of wills began. The Scouts informed me that the previous Scoutmaster always brought a camp chef and that he cooked all the food for them. My answer was, "Hmm, that's interesting, I don't think that is the Scouting way." I paused and then added. "And I am not your mom". I was getting my information from my copy of the Scoutmaster handbook, 1932 edition. The program calls for them to cook their own food. My thought was that there was no better time than tonight to begin the practice.

"How do we peel potatoes?" they yelled out.

"With a knife", I replied.

I heard weeping and gnashing of teeth as some were peeling potatoes and building a campfire for the first time. They were upset at the idea of having to do for themselves. They were overly accustomed to being catered to. All of this was about to change. I was not prepared though, for the rants and tantrums that soon followed.

Seth, the Scout in charge of the fire, had never used a flint-n-steel. In the past, they had used matches and gasoline, also known as "Scout juice," to get their fires going. Building a fire without the use of these dangerous methods was frustrating to Seth. My challenge to start a fire using only his flint, steel and items found in nature was nearly more than he could bear. He pretty much lost it at the thought of such a task. He then spent nearly four hours getting a fire going.

"Can't we just use Scout juice?" He questioned.

"No!" was my response -firmly.

For those who are not Scouters, Scout juice refers to the use of an accelerant, such as gasoline for lighting a fire. This was something that I vowed never to do as a Scoutmaster. An idea that I came across while studying Baden Powell, the founder of Scouting. Early Scouts had to "make fire" using primitive means or anything that they could find in nature. I found this to be a novel idea and sound advice, so I put it into play. Our Scouts would not use any commercial means, paper, lighters or GASOLINE to aide them in their efforts. My resolve may have been strengthened by the vivid images of me burning my sister's eyebrows off when we were kids.

It was well after dark when we finally had enough coals to place the large cast iron skillet on the fire to begin cooking. We had scarcely begun doing so when Wiley, cooking for the first time, attempting to turn the fried potatoes, used the spatula like a bulldozer and scooped them out of the skillet into the fire.

He immediately quit cooking. He ran off and got into his dad's car. His emotional outburst produced real tears and he displayed frustration. I found myself on the precipice of a choice that would affect my own attitude of Scouting for years to come. He screamed that dinner was ruined and that *he couldn't do it*. He said it was just too difficult. Agh! He used those magic words. "I quit, I can't." Somehow when I hear those words, they trigger something inside of me, that says, oh, yes you can. And I'll show you how.

My own father never let me quit. He allowed us to choose, but once the choice was made, he would then make sure that you saw it through to the end. We learned to make better choices and to finish what we started. You might fail in the attempt, but quitting was never acceptable. He also taught us that chores, like cooking, taking out the trash, or feeding the animals were not choices, but necessities of life. You simply had to do them because you breathe air and are part of a family. One might say that he thought that completing chores was part of the cost of living.

I gave Wiley a few minutes to shake it off. Refusing to accept defeat, I then followed him to the car where I began to make annoying sounds outside of the car. I kept going until I broke his tantrum and gained his attention. I then explained that I refused to accept his resignation. I also explained to him my plans to sit outside of the car and make obnoxious noises. He was free to choose to sit in the car and be miserable or he could choose to come and have another go of it. His dad eye rolled my method. The choice was his to make.

My hope and the need that I felt was to coach him to success instead of accepting the failure. It would have been easier just to let him go. But I was afraid that accepting his quitting would send the message that it was okay to give up when the going becomes difficult or uncomfortable.

This is written in my handbook, it's part of who I am. Though this episode was the first of several with Wiley, in time I realized that it was a common thread with many of today's youth. If it isn't easy, they just quit or won't do it. The value system that they operate from is not one of deciding what is best or for the greater good. Rather it is one that decides, to do or not to do a thing, based on difficulty or level of comfort. This is one of the results of parents always fighting their battles for them.

Wiley needed a win here and I wanted him to win, enough that I was determined to show him how. I firmly believe that the best path is to encourage them through the storm or challenge, not to remove it.

As I walked to the emotional edge with Wiley, it was my hope to talk him back down. As I stood there outside of that car making those noises, I was relieved when he finally relented, deciding that another attempt to cook was less painful than sitting and listening to me. His change of heart was timely, as my desire to continue with my obnoxious act was waning.

Wiley quickly learned that all was not lost, that he was better than this, and that we expected more from him. We simply started over with new potatoes and helped him succeed, successfully cooking his portion of dinner that night. He learned or rather experienced, that he can.

It was not the last time that he tested my resolve or the limits of the expectations that were set. I saw a small change in Wiley, that began that night, which continued to grow for several years, until I was there at his Eagle Court of Honor.

Over the next several months he grew emotionally, and his self-esteem became validated, and secure with an increased ability to overcome and to do. He simply needed to know that we were there for him and that it was okay, to make some mistakes. It is all part of how we learn.

The stars were long out, and the mountain chill had set in before we ate that night. Our dinner was okay and consisted of a skillet chicken, not quite melted Velveeta cheese and semi raw fried potatoes. We were hungry enough to make the undercooked meal seem, ever so palatable.

Round two began at sunrise the next morning. The day was filled with familiar Scout activities, namely eating, hiking and having a little fun. Our breakfast consisted of bacon and deep-fried pancakes, because Matt dumped half a bottle of cooking oil into the skillet as he was cooking them. Even through all the mistakes, I've never had them prepared in such a manner since. It became just one of the many unique cuisines that the Scouts would introduce me to.

As we began our activities, we came across a freshly half-eaten sheep on our Geo Cache run and subsequently chased a cougar for a few yards up the mountain. As they were chasing the cougar off, it occurred to them that they were chasing a COUGAR! I was beyond relief and silently happy when it deescalated as quickly as it had begun. A couple of caches were found for practice and then we created one called "Oh, Snatch." We rounded the morning out with a 10-mile hike.

Then came lunch. I can still hear their words as they asked how they were going to cook their hotdogs. At least it didn't require four or five hours to get the fire going. Seth became more resourceful at starting a fire overnight.

He recently reminded me that he found joy, as he used some leftover coals to start the new fire. Unfortunately, the coals that he is referring to, were the ones that should have been extinguished completely after breakfast.

"Hey, Scoutmaster, where are your hotdog cookers?" The Scouts asked.

"I didn't bring any, the woods are full of them." I answered.

"What do you mean?" they asked.

Me: "Look around, there are thousands of them. Pick one." There were some huffing and puffing and then some Scouts began to figure it out. I sat there watching them with a chuckle. These boys, these Scouts, had never used a stick, as in a real stick to cook a hotdog. How can that be?

Some fully believed that they had to have a hotdog cooker, a commercially made stick to cook their dogs over the open fire. They had never experienced it otherwise. They could not think outside of the box, yet.

Then it started, "Well, I'm not going to eat then."

"Ok" I answered, "Don't eat."

It wasn't that I really didn't want them to eat, it was just that I wasn't going to cave to the demand. I thought to myself, "A Scout won't die if he misses just one meal, right?"

"If we don't have a stove, and we don't have a pan of water, how do we cook them?" they continued.

I then demonstrated how to select a stick, prep it with my pocketknife and then cook a hotdog over the fire. I watched as a few attempted to stick their hotdogs over sticks that were larger in diameter than their hotdogs. It was a painful experience to observe for me and the hotdog.

But then this is Scouting, to teach them to do difficult things, to develop character, through experiences, to teach youth to make moral and ethical decisions throughout their lifetimes by instilling into them the Scouting Ideals as found in the Scout Oath and Scout Law.

During this outing, I observed that their equipment load was extreme and overbearing. For an overnight camp, we don't all need a 6-man tent, air mattress, chair, blanket, sleeping bag, pillow, three coats and three changes of clothing, a bag of snacks from mom, and a cell phone. I am sure that we had more gear than Bear Grylls, though not as fancy. These tents weren't just any old tents, they were Springbar tents, which weigh about 80 pounds.

Okay, the three changes of clothing may have been an exaggeration, but you get the point. We just don't need all that heavy cumbersome gear for an overnighter. It was stressful to worry about and to transport. We needed to strip down, before the next outing. We needed to learn to do with less.

A great deal of time was spent not only setting up the gear but worrying about all the stuff. Oh, and when it came time to pack it all up, I got schooled in the need to prioritize the departure proceedings. Feeding them first, and then asking them to pack it up and clean it up, was an experience in patience.

Note for next outing: The obvious thing here is to bring less stuff. The second item I discovered was that it is best to hold out on what they want most, until you have completed your mission. For us, this meant keeping lunch in the ready while they packed. Once their little bellies were filled, attempting to get them to pack up was futile. The third item on my list is no more car camping. Car camping is the habit of pulling up somewhere and camping next to the car. The idea is that this requires very little effort. I find this a contradiction to what we are attempting to model and teach. The habit keeps one from going to more challenging and rewarding places.

The Scouts appreciate things more, when they have some skin in the game. Hiking to the campsite, for example provides this.

The outing was a great opportunity for the Scouts, Kevin (assistant SM) and I to get to know each other. We still laugh about trying to shove the stick, larger in diameter than the Hot Dog, into the Hot Dog and watching it break apart. It seems funny now and still gives me a chuckle or two. However, at the time, real tears of frustration were spent that afternoon learning how to 'stick a dog' to cook it.

Every good leader needs a sidekick. Kevin, the 'Happy Bear,' as the Scouts referred to him, was mine. Kevin is as old-school grit and vinegar as they come. He is just stubborn enough that he won't back down and he, too, helps them to see things through.

On this outing, he used a giant cube-shaped magnifying lens to make a fire. The Scouts were fascinated with this experiment. I noted how they seemed to love for us to show them how, to give them new information.

At the conclusion of camp, Kevin revealed that he had several old fire extinguishers. If you have ever wanted to pull the tab and give one a squeeze, we did, and it was fun. It filled the area with powder that looked like smoke. It was the only time in my life, that I have "extinguished" a campfire, and oh, so thoroughly. We emptied all of them onto the fire and coals in the firepit. I'm sorry, Seth, no coals to start the next one. This time they were dead cold and out.

WE ARE CAPABLE OF FAR MORE THAN WE KNOW.

Our boys are far more capable than they know, we just need to help them see it.

We need to expect more from them.

Paul Fowler

3 ARE WE THERE, YET?

Our next excursion was in the heat of June. Kevin and I had decided to take the boys on a "real" outing. That meant ditching the car and hiking to our camp. We arrived at the agreed meeting place and began our journey up Waterfall Canyon above Ogden, Utah.

The trip was eerily like taking a long road trip in a car full of chipmunks. I am pretty sure the words, "Are we there yet?" have never been spoken so many times in such a short span of time.

The hike started out gentle and flat. As we journeyed along our way, the terrain quickly changed and began to be increasingly more aggressive.

As we progressed the steps began to be more up than out. At this point, my hamstrings and my gluteus maximus were getting the workout of a lifetime by carrying the overloaded backpack up the rock face of that mountain.

It was mid-June and it was hot and sweaty. An icy cold mountain stream ran along the path, just out of sight. The sound of the stream gurgling and crackling through the rocks seemed to be mocking our thirst.

As we journeyed, the Scouts were becoming increasingly more creative in their attempts to get us to stop and camp along the way. I am sure that there was more than one plea of, "Let's camp here and finish going up tomorrow."

The areas that they were suggesting in their desperate attempts to persuade us to stop were not big enough for us all to stand, let alone pitch not one, but at least three tents.

Devon, who weighed in at maybe 85 pounds, was carrying a backpack of about the same weight. To quote Seth, "It must be about

1000 pounds!" Devon was struggling severely and Kevin and I each carried extra water and food just in case someone forgot or didn't bring enough. I will mention here that that was one of the dumbest things I have done as a Scoutmaster. Not only did Kevin and I carry too much, the Scouts all had extra stuff from their moms. In addition to their meal rations, they had extra water, jerky, sugary snacks and even some canned goods. Yes, canned goods on a hiking trip! All these just added to the difficulty of climbing up that mountain.

Some better planning and pack inspections would have saved much effort and most likely reduced the intensity of the leg cramps that followed. I would have gladly dropped ten or even thirty pounds from my backpack, had I known about the surplus that we were all carrying.

The ascent was interesting enough as we came across the Swat Team Training camp, complete with a climbing wall and a stash box for their climbing gear. There were several foot bridges that crossed the stream and I loved hearing the sound of bubbling waters. The trail continued crisscrossing the stream as we made the ascent to the falls.

The overgrown brush made it difficult to see up the trail. The twist and turns finished off any hope of viewing what lie ahead of us. As we progressed, the trail become more rock-laden and steep.

There was a steady flow of people making their way down the mountain as we were climbing up, so much so that we had to step off the path several times to let them pass. They all had such encouraging words like, "Oh, you have a way to go," or, "I hope you make it okay with those packs. We barely made it with our water bottles." Or the classic encouragement, "We never made it all the way. We turned back. It was more difficult that we ever imagined."

As I worked to motivate the Scouts, I remember using the words, "it's just a little further," mixed with their famous Scout words, "are we there yet?" repeated over and over what to me seemed to be hundreds of times.

We stopped several times along the journey to rest and hydrate. At this point, rather than sit, I preferred to lean on my hiking stick as it became increasing more difficult to get up after sitting down. I was becoming well acquainted and appreciative of my hiking stick. I now considered him my best friend on the trip.

Among our challenges was the fact that Kevin is a diabetic, so the excursion for him was a real struggle. The constant climb was draining on our energy. We had to wait for Kevin a few times and I had doubts he would arrive at the top with us. We paused a few times to feed him Snickers bars. He was truly struggling. I was concerned about his health and ability to gut it up the hill. In the end, Kevin proved that he still had some salt.

The Scouts didn't know that their new Scoutmaster was motivated by challenges and the words "It can't be done." So, the more they complained, the more determined I became at accomplishing the ascent to the waterfall.

I coached them on. I used every inspiring phrase that I possessed to motivate them to complete the climb. I felt that if they saw that I could do it, they would know that they could. I did not want to force them, and yet I could not accept giving up or quitting. I knew that they needed to make it to the top. I was also quietly hoping that it would all be worth the effort when we got there.

By dinner time we made it! We reached the top! I was relieved to see the waterfall. It was sweltering hot and the cool spraying mist felt good on our overheated bodies. The view of the 100-foot waterfall and the overlook of the valley below, was well worth the climb.

The next words that I spoke were, "Don't climb on the rocks!" The next thing I observed was the Scouts climbing the rocks!

I looked back over my shoulder to see if I could see Kevin. He was behind and below us far enough that he was now out of sight. Some time passed before he came into view. The Scouts ran down and helped him carry his pack into camp.

We cooked our dinners using our mess kits and camp stoves. It was at this time that we discovered that the Scouts had all carried too much food and extras to eat. We had more food than we could possibly eat. Too many moms were afraid that their sons were going to starve, I suppose.

I once read a statistic that claimed that no Scout has ever actually starved to death at any camp, ever! What, to me, was the bigger danger, was dying from the exhaustion caused by carrying all the extra weight of the cans and bottles of the unneeded food and water.

I know that we shouldn't feed wildlife. But at this moment, I would gladly have fed a bear, maybe even two of them, squirrels and even some racoons, to not have to lug around all the extra weight anymore.

As our bellies were filled with our gourmet camp chow, we began putting up our tents. I was contemplating how we were going to sleep on the shards of rock at the base of the waterfall. I called out to the Scouts to not pitch their tents too close to the falling water or the mist would soak them during the night.

The sun was setting opposite the waterfall and the scene was a beauty to behold, it was at this point that I began to realize that this spot was some form of lover's lane. As darkness settled around us, so too did the couples up from the University below. Who would have thought this? Well, certainly not this Scoutmaster. Still determined to have some degree of privacy and to avoid exposing the Scouts to their less than scrupulous behavior, Kevin and I began to have several loud conversations between our tents to drown out the sounds of the other visitors and, in our own way, encourage them to move on up the trail.

A side story to this outing was Kevin getting a new "thrifty" style tent. Kevin had explained to his wife that, since he was a Scout leader, he needed some additional gear. She had agreed and said that she would pick up a new tent for him. I can only assume that her sense of thrift overcame her as she priced out new equipment. She may even have been flabbergasted at the cost and made a choice based on those feelings.

Whatever the reasons were, Kevin was the recipient of her thrift. Being the good sport that he is, I don't recall any complaints from him.

I have a picture of what can only be described as a highway workers body bag. We may have even poked Kevin in the morning, just to be sure that he was still with us. He lay inside of an orange tube emergency tent, soaked from the condensation.

I wish that Kevin was the only one that had equipment issues that night. Though I did have a nice tent, my issue was the "summer" sleeping bag that I purchased for the journey. I had grown tired of my usual sleeping bag. It has served me well for several decades. It was heavy and cumbersome, and I wasn't fond of the idea of hiking with it. I went to a local retailer and explained that I needed a summertime backpacking bag. The clerk showed me the perfect sleeping bag to meet my needs, so he said.

I purchased it and brought it along on this trip without even a thought. That night as I crawled into my tent, I discovered that the new light weight sleeping bag was designed for someone much smaller than myself. It fit like a shirt that was four sizes too small. I could not even fit it around myself. And as for padding for sleeping on those rocks, I should have just carried a spare towel along; it would've provided more comfort.

That night, as I lay in my tent, I suffered through what would become the first of many unexplained, intense leg pains. As I sipped my water, I was unable to straighten my legs.

After breakfast, we prepared for our journey back down the trail.

Amazingly, the Scouts were able to cover the distance back down to the parking lot, in what seemed to be minutes, and without any issues or complaints!

I began to notice the badge of courage as the boys conquered difficult challenges.

Their body language tells me that they feel better about themselves when they complete challenges. And each unique challenge once conquered, makes them a little more unique and a little stronger.

THE MANTRA OF "All in or Not at All".

This is how we approach all our activities and the last words that we spoke as we parted from any gathering of Troop #210.

Why try or bother to make half attempts at getting something done? If we start, then we finish. It reminded us that we, as in ALL of us, are in. We include everyone. We're like family and help each other to succeed.

We are All in or Not at All!

We end each gathering or event with a kneeling prayer. We gather into an all-inclusive circle, knuckle bump and then yell the words, "All in or Not at All!"

4 BUILD IT.
THEY WILL COME.

As the next month rolled around, I continued keeping my commitment to go camping with Troop #210, every month. July was approaching and the theme was "Scout Summer Camp". There were no plans or arrangements from the previous leader, so the slate was open. I soon discovered that there were no openings this late in the season in the traditional camps in our area. This presented a second challenge in finding a location to hold our summer camp.

Like many of you, I suffer from several anxieties. As a result, I sometimes can spiral into a series of endless possibilities or thoughts. I can over analyze situations to the point of becoming paralyzed, or unable to decide.

One of the ways I manage these anxieties, is that I instinctively avoid new places and food from unknown sources. I manage them, through routines, that were about to get disrupted.

My wife likes to remind me, that no matter where we are, I always seem to know where the exit is. While it is true that I don't like to be boxed in, it really isn't a fear of the unknown so much as a desire to know where I am going, where the toilet facilities are, and that the food won't make me sick.

As I contemplated camp; these anxieties kicked into overdrive. My mind ran away with endless thoughts and possibilities and all the worries of potential failure. Yes, it became paralyzing.

I truly wanted to follow through on being the right type of Scoutmaster and go with the boys and make sure they had their summer camp. In contrast to my desire to do the right thing, the fear –

or anxiety – of going to the unknown was unbearable to me. I did not want to go. I did not feel that I could be away for such a long period of time. I was sleepless. I broke out in a sweat at the idea. Going to camp, to the unknown, the fear of not being good enough, and to be away from work, all were stressful challenges for me to overcome.

As I struggled immensely with this, I spent time on my knees having conversations with God about my concerns. I didn't know how to do a Scout camp. I had never been away from my businesses for more than a day or two at a time. I was worried about all the issues that would present themselves in my absence. I was stressed and overwhelmed with the details of just how to put this camp together. Additionally, there was the fear of failure. Though I was a Scout with camping experience, I never had the opportunity to attend a summer camp, as a youth nor as an adult.

While I was struggling and pouring my heart out to God, a thought like a voice came to my mind that said, "Build it. They will come." And, "If you organize the camp, the boys will attend." I felt peace with that thought and my anxieties leveled off. I knew that I needed to move forward.

I promised God that I would take the leap of faith and organize the camp for the Scouts, that I would go and be with them. I asked HIM for a blessing, in return, if it was his will, that he would help me with my anxieties and my business concerns. I prayed that my business, my livelihood, my source of income, would be successful in my absence.

Being self-employed, I don't have paid vacations. I had never been away from my business for a week at a time. Whenever I am gone, even for a day or two, I spend much of my time responding to emails, text and needed phone calls. I am never away.

This time was different. The boys needed my attention and I wanted to give it to them 100%. I was truly willing to give these boys all that I had, all that I am. Doing these events would come at a great cost to myself. Confronting my anxieties was a reality with which I had to contend.

How was I going to be able to do this? I haven't had the resources to take my family on a week's vacation in decades, and now I was expected to leave it all behind and take someone else's kids for a week. It was truly a test of my faith in God and my commitment to HIM.

I set out to Do My Best, to Do My Duty. I began to read and to pray for guidance. I asked forgiveness for my earlier hard feelings about Scouting. I took an instructor training course. I registered as a Merit Badge counselor. I researched Merit Badges that we might be able to do and began to piece together the resources to bring those classes to fruition.

Over the course of the summer that same small voice said to me:

➢ "If you want the Scouts to follow, you must be going (leading) somewhere."
➢ "It is hard to follow something that isn't moving."
➢ "Do it. They will come and follow." (meaning arrange the camp)
➢ "No car camping. Go do real camping, it will change them."
➢ "It is not important where you camp. Just do it."
➢ "Make service a part of your program."
➢ "Focus on what, not where, and have a 'why' for each outing."
➢ "Love the boys but challenge them. Cause them to stretch."
➢ "Help them to recognize my Spirit and influence. Teach them to follow it."

The things that we needed for a successful camp fell into place. The people, the equipment, the training, and of course, the Scouts, all came together as if guided by an unseen hand.

All of the Scouts in our unit attended the camp, with a few extras.

We held a successful camp with no causalities and plenty of unique experiences and stories to tell.

5 CAMP FOWLER

I felt more than inspired to put the camp together. I felt guided through the process of creating our camp. The ideas and opportunities came together in a fluid-like manner. It seemed as if everything that we needed was there in a timely fashion.

I spoke with my parents, then living in Ferron, Utah, and we decided that taking the Scouts to their little horse ranch would be a good idea.

I arranged for us to stay at Millsite State Park in Ferron, Utah. I converted our land yacht into a Scoutmaster lodge and the camp resource center. I contacted my best friend, DJ Bott, and roped him and his brother Mike into helping with camp. Mike was a certified (BSA approved) Canoe Merit Badge instructor. DJ had previously served as a Scoutmaster in our church troop.

In a way, getting him involved in helping with the camp was a payback as he and Larry Hawkes had been involved in doing the rope-a-dope on me to get me to become a Scoutmaster.

The Wynn Family in Ferron would also help us with the horses. They were National Rodeo Champions and had incredibly well-trained horses. As for horsemanship, the Scouts were in for a treat.

I continued to pray for guidance, as well as the faith to follow through with this. I expressed gratitude to God and that I trusted HIM and the inspiration and guidance that I was receiving. It was truly a step into the darkness for me. My faith in Him was all I had to go on. After lots of struggling, I received the impression and thought to not worry, that all would be well with my home and business concerns during my absence.

God was working a miracle within me as I continued to work on behalf of these young men. HE was showing me how important these boys were to HIM and how much they will be needed in the coming days on earth. He was changing my heart, and as a result, me.

I became acutely aware that there's a vacuum of leaders for these boys. A tragedy, considering that this is a critical time in their maturation, a time when they are learning what a man is and should be. This is a vulnerable time for them. They're choosing whether to follow the world or to follow the teachings of Christ.

My testimony that I was on the Lord's errand began to grow as I worked with these boys. I felt that Scouting was a tool that we were given to use, not the goal. Becoming an Eagle should be a natural consequence of Scouting, not the objective.

I spent time on my knees thanking God and asking for HIS guidance. I knew I needed the help and inspiration. I was not shy about turning to the one who knows us all and who knows our needs. I spent hours on my knees seeking answers and asking the key question of, "What would HE have me do, in regard to these young men?"

I learned firsthand that while you are in the service of others, God will readily inspire you. When the answers came, I learned I needed to act and to not ask, unless I was prepared to act. This is when I really began to develop a passion for teaching these young men.

The camp proceeded much like a typical summer camp, with some exceptions for more structure and direct input from an inexperienced and obsessed Scoutmaster.

We had merit badge classes and instruction in Canoeing, Rifle, Horsemanship, Cooking, and other various Scouter crafts. The Scouts prepared their own meals and completed several service projects.

On one of the days during camp, they were working with Granddad (my father) on their Horsemanship Merit Badge. That Tuesday, several of them skipped the studying and tried to B.S. their way through the class. It was then that I noticed they were about to flint granddad off. The very moment I turned to share my observation with DJ, Granddad paused, took his finger, and pointed at them as he said firmly, "You boys don't know s#$%! Now, before I waste any more of my time, get over there and do your homework. Read the material and make an effort to learn. When you are ready, come back over and we will continue."

I believe that was exactly what they needed to hear at that moment in time. They snapped out of their squirrel mode with a stunned look on their faces and returned to crack open the books, with a new level of discipline.

As we returned to camp for lunch, we found that we had been raided by chipmunks. During their invasion, they had opened a Planter's Nuts can using the type of speed and finesse that even Flash Gordon would be envious of.

Earlier that day we had the conversation about, "No food in the tents!" Now, some of the Scouts had firsthand knowledge of why we didn't want food in their tents.

It was at this moment that Wiley came forth, obviously distraught, and complained that they (chipmunks) had eaten all his chocolate and peanuts.

Those little demons had chewed into the canvas tent and ate the lip off his gallon-sized Planter's trail mix can, consuming all the chocolate and nuts. At about that same moment, we found a chipmunk on a hill nearby, probably to watch if we had more. It felt like mockery. Emotional outburst number two, check.

The second flint with Granddad came after lunch that day. Some of them were too timid at scraping the poo from the horse's hooves. Granddad replied, "Don't be a wimp, it's just horse poop. Now get in there and get it scraped out!"

He was not allowing them to take this class by audit and observation. He was requiring full participation – practical exercise! Strangely, I was being entertained by the engagement between them. He was getting them physically involved.

As we worked the Horsemanship Merit Badge, the Scouts kept requesting to ride the pony, my fiery daughters' horse. Some of the Scouts were intimidated by the size of the other horses. Unlike the Scouts, granddad judged the horses by temperament more than size. He attempted to explain this and asked them to not ride the pony, several times. He further explained the reasons why. He repeated the request to let the pony be and to focus on the horses. They still seemed to be drawn to the pony. They continued to persist, I suppose, thinking that the pony would be an easier, less intimidating ride for them. After a time, he relented by allowing them to attempt to ride the smaller, more mischievous animal. They attempted to ride the pony and were bucked off. Now, they had a firsthand experience and an understanding that all things are not always as they appear to be.

There is no teacher like experience, and I know of no better place than the farm to gain this experience. They now listened more intensely, as he taught them not just how to ride, but how to read and to interact with the horse. By the end of our time, none of them, it seemed, wanted to leave the horses.

By Thursday, the Scouts were wearing down, most likely because they were running out of sugar from home. Their appetites were fueling up and their malleability was on the rise. This is the best part of any camp with the Scouts. This is the moment of impact and learning.

Thursday was our day for service and a planned privation. Privations are something that I love to use. Something that I discovered by accident, that helps make boys into men.

We set out Thursday morning with a dam hike. As part of giving back, we had volunteered to clean up a considerable length of shoreline at the Millsite Reservoir. The dam hike was our opportunity to clean up the trash and debris from the campground over to the dam. This was a new level of challenge for the Scouts who were accustomed to working in time slots, like fifteen or thirty minutes, versus going until the job is done – all day if needed.

The water in the reservoir was exceptionally low so there was plenty of uneven shoreline exposed, making the trek along its edge even more challenging and tiring. We were hiking up and down and in and out of the inlets, over and over.

As we hiked along picking up trash, I received a constant barrage of, "how much further is it?" "Oh, we are just working our way over to the dam", I said.

"Where is it?"

"Oh, just around a corner and a few hundred more yards." I said to the Scouts.

As we would clear the next inlet and go around the next corner, the same question was asked, to which the same answer was always given, perhaps a hundred times. Each time their impatience would grow somewhat as we would discuss the difference between around "this corner" and what I had actually said - around "a corner". They were not finding humor in my word play. And I was not stopping until we completed the task.

The trash bags were filling up fast and becoming difficult to manage as we hiked up and around and down the uneven shoreline. Finally, a Scout let loose with a full-on meltdown. We paused to allow the smoke to clear and then continued to complete the task at hand.

The Scouts were relieved when we arrived at the dumpsite shortly after and then hiked back to camp.

After lunch, in the heat of the day, we continued work on an additional service project by making repairs and enhancements to the landscaping at the park. By dinner time, the Scouts were pretty much spent. Most of the day had passed by doing service projects and hiking.

With all the work complete, we announced to the Scouts that they had some free time to which there was much jubilation. During their free time, we, the leaders, set to work on preparing our best meal and requested that they come to dinner at the appropriate time, cleaned up and dressed in full uniform.

DJ, Mike and I spent the next few hours cooking BBQ Chicken, Cheesy Potatoes, Triple Chocolate-Raspberry cake, and Caesar salad - the works.

When the meal was ready, we gathered around and served the boys up. We wanted to show them that we, too, did chores and did them well. We were happy to do the same things that we expected from them.

They ate and enjoyed themselves. We presented them with new patrol neckerchiefs. It was a moment of connection. We had purposely, pushed them hard throughout the day and now the boys were malleable and calm.

We next traveled over to Emery Co and hiked up past the petroglyphs. As we did so we challenged the boys to remain as quiet as possible and to tell us later what they had felt and observed.

We discussed the reality of people living here before and, even though we couldn't see them today, that they were none the less real. Grandma Jan related stories of her childhood about the Chiefs and the peoples that had lived there while she was growing up. She explained the petroglyphs.

She made the connection between what we can see and what we cannot, explaining that even though we cannot see a thing, it does not make it any less real. Seeing and touching the petroglyphs helped make these earlier Native Americans real to the Scouts. We looked around for other evidences of their civilization.

After a brief time discussing ancient peoples, we continued our hike up the mountain. The Scouts were quiet and observant. They were worn down enough physically that they were being quite pleasant, and, at this very moment, they were teachable – even malleable. By design, this was what we had been working for.

It seemed as if someone was guiding us along. There was a feeling in the air that said, "you are not alone." This was a sacred moment in our experience at this camp.

We followed the trail until we arrived at the pinnacle. The pinnacle was a perfect point splitting the valley and river below into a "Y" intersection. We could look down either valley. As we did so, we let our imaginations run away a little as we envisioned the life of these earlier residents.

The boys began to express what they were feeling and experiencing. It was a powerful moment that had been created by the privations and challenges of the days leading up to this point in time. We were away from all the man-made distractions, and it felt as if God was there with us. The boys were very open as we discussed what they felt good about in their lives and what they didn't. The conversation was powerful and moving. The planned hardships and service (privations) that we had put them through had taken their effect. It was rewarding for me to have the boys openly share their feelings, beliefs and experiences. This was the highlight of 'Camp Fowler'.

During the week, we had been building up stories of wolves and cougars. While hiking, we had pointed out several of the large animal tracks in the area.

As Friday rolled around, it was time for the Scouts to do their wilderness survival. This meant spending a night outside of camp, no tent and no adults.

As fate would have it, the anxieties created from the wildlife stories kept them huddled, like a pile of puppies, together during the night of their 'survival' in the wilderness.

Observing them returning Saturday morning, one could readily see the badge of courage that they now proudly displayed.

The week of camp had been physically and mentally challenging for the Scouts. The week had left an impression upon these young souls. Fears had been faced down as they worked on the Canoeing, Wilderness Survival and Horsemanship merit badges. They had experienced both frustration and jubilation. They had some failures and some successes. The mountain experience left an indelible impression as they felt and connected with Heaven. And of course, we all had plenty of laughs, too!

Notes for the next camp: 1. No chocolate for Scouts in the summer, especially in the vehicles. 2. Moms pack too much stuff. 3. Scouts won't eat until they deplete the sugary treats, they brought from home.

6 BAD WATER
You want to be able to say that you never gave up, that you did do your best!

Our next camp came as a new Assistant Scoutmaster, Doug Gilbert, joined our group. This time, our journey took us to Antelope Island. During the planning for this camp, we contacted the U.S. Forestry Service and the Bureau of Land Management looking for conservation projects that we could perform. It had been suggested that we offer our services to prepare the bison corrals for the upcoming auction to be held on Antelope Island.

We had been working through the summer on the Cycling Merit Badge. Cycling is a great challenge for many Scouts, especially those that are younger or less athletic. It is also one of the required options for the Eagle Scout Rank.

Our troop's plan was to camp on Antelope Island, complete our service project and then finish up by riding a 25-miler bike ride. It would be a triple header.

It was a typical August with all the heat and humidity that you would expect. Even so, we were determined to not let the heat keep us from continuing our journey to complete an outing each month.

Kevin was to be the chase and pit crew vehicle during the bike ride. Doug and I would be riding along with the Scouts, attempting to keep them within eyesight of each other. We felt that we had all our bases covered.

This camp seemed to be progressing more smoothly. We had more experience and the Scouts were learning where the bar of expectation was. They were beginning to take charge and becoming more independent.

Our Friday night passed uneventfully. We didn't have any meltdowns, and I don't recall any tantrums. The Scouts cooked their hot dogs over the campfire without any blow back or issues. We didn't have any equipment failures. It seemed to be calm, even boring. I prematurely mused to myself about how smoothly this camp was progressing. Everyone was participating. We were enjoying the time. The food was good, and the atmosphere was relaxed.

Saturday morning, we ate, filled our water bottles and headed over to the Bison Stalls on our bikes. We worked for several hours in the hot sun cleaning the stalls and pulling weeds. We had a grand time of it, piling the debris that we removed from the stalls. I can't say that the Scouts were thrilled about this portion of the day, but they were working, nonetheless. Midway through the project, we had our first tantrum and walk off. For some, engaging in physical labor is an extreme challenge, sadly, not something they are used to. But this type of activity or privation sometimes sets the stage for the deeper experiences and learning that we desire these boys to have.

With the service project in the bag, our next goal was to complete a 25-mile bike ride. We headed out across the Island to the lower side on our bikes. It was now mid-day and the sun was blistering hot. There is no shade to be found anywhere on Antelope island. We were headed down to the Bison for a visit and then return to our campsite on the high side of the Island.

As the Scouts like to tell it, "It was one hundred and three degrees in the shade." I'm not sure that it ever broke 100 degrees, but it is true that It was hot and humid, and that we were now riding into the hottest part of the day.

Another Scout dad had joined us for this camp out. Our journey had scarcely begun when he was having us stop for water. It seemed that we were stopping every couple hundred yards. This simple 25-mile ride would take us most of the day at this rate.

I questioned to myself, "Is this real? Do we really need to rest and hydrate every few minutes, or does he need to be shown how to win?"

There is always a need to emphasize safety, and then there is just pushing it to the point of stalling and damming progress.

I decided to push on to keep the boys moving along. I was attempting to balance between the necessary hydration and getting the job done. To push too far to either side was to invite disaster. Not enough hydration combined with too much exertion could bring heat exhaustion.

At the same time, too much emphasis on hydration and not exerting oneself also brings on disaster. That being, that we inadvertently teach these boys to not do difficult things. We literally teach them not to achieve; to not do the difficult or challenging.

Why is it that hills always seem to be much steeper and longer when you are peddling?

As we neared the halfway point in our journey, Seth became very ill. He was off his bike and puking on the roadside.

I pulled up alongside him and waited as he gained some degree of composure. He wanted to quit. He and I had an exchange while I waited for him to compose himself. After a brief period, we walk along slowly while he cooled off.

I then said to him, "Seth, you can quit, and no one will blame you. It is hot. You are ill. It is okay and you can get a ride back to camp in Kevin's truck. But Seth, you and I know that months or years from now, it will bother you if you do so today."

"I don't care," he said.

And then, "I'm sick."

"It isn't fair, I am sorry for that" I added.

"You want to be able to say that you never gave up, that you completed this ride, even though you were sick. You want to DO your BEST. You want to be able to say that you gave it your all and you succeeded."

And further, "It will haunt you if you quit even though it sucks."

Lastly, "You want to be able to tell this story at a future place and time, about how you succeeded. You will know what it feels like to win, in the face of adversity."

We waited a few minutes longer. He walked alongside his bike for a time. He sipped down more water and then got on his bike and rode away. At that moment, I could not have been more well pleased with Seth.

We had consumed most of our water by the time we arrived at the lower ranger station. We inquired about more drinking water and the ranger instructed us where we could reload our jugs with 'safe water'.

We were then permitted to go out on foot among the bison. As we did so, we gained an appreciation for their immense size. Even at a small distance, we realized that they were as large as, and most likely weigh more than a car.

The Scouts and I discussed how to read animals and to be safe around them.

We took a break to cool off and then began our journey back to camp. Yes, it really was up hill all the way back to camp. Regardless the Scouts started back to camp with a vigorous pace, leaving me well behind. They were on their way back to camp and nothing it seemed was going to stop or slow them down. To them, the end was in sight.

As we peddled back to camp, we drank our water from the ranger. We should have noticed that it had a strange chlorine taste to it. Several of the Scouts became ill after drinking it.

I caught up with them on the last hill, near the end of our journey, when Wiley gave out. He was done. He was quitting and he didn't care. He was physically spent and overheating in the hot sun. His face was flushed. I knew that he was most likely experiencing heat exhaustion. I also knew it was important to be able to finish.

I explained to him that we couldn't quit. That as Scouts we just weren't wired to do that. But that didn't mean that we had to ride all the way either. I met him halfway on this one. He needed to cool off. I promised that if he wouldn't give up, I would walk beside him. So, we walked along – up hill mind you. All that was important at that moment was that we were still moving along. "Just keep moving forward, making progress. Even if it means one foot at a time, let's keep moving."

He walked along for some time as he leaned over on his bike and watched the pebbles pass by.

Seth was next to want to give up. Acknowledging to them that their bikes weren't of the best caliber nor the easiest to ride distance with served no useful purpose. So, I complimented them on their bikes. My thinking is that **one needs to win or lose without handicaps or excuses.**

The heat and exertion were having their effect on me. I too, was near to passing out. What was in that water from the ranger? A headache, nausea, fatigue? What were these sensations telling me?

I worked to slow my breathing and to calm my body and heart rate. We continued to move along at a snail's pace, allowing our bodies to cool down and dissipate some of the heat. The August sun was bearing down on us hard. It felt somewhat like a sauna.

We kept moving forward, one step at a time, never giving up, never letting into the temptation to quit. At some point, each of them found their wind and energy, mounted their bikes and rode off to camp, leaving me to continue my journey alone. At that very moment, I was longing for the energies of youth. I coveted how quickly their bodies recovered and sprang back to life.

I made it back to camp and rested for a time in the shade as they (the Scouts and Kevin) broke camp and loaded up our bikes in the trailer. On the way to camp, I recognized the seriousness of the situation, I had stopped sweating and I was in a state of dizziness and feeling nausea. Heat exhaustion can be a serious scenario, but I could not let the Scouts see me quit. I pushed on slowly, attempting to limit my exertion, placing myself in low-energy mode to allow my body to recuperate as best it may. I sipped water, slowly. I worked at slowing my heart rate down, by concentrating and using deep breaths. We all made it safely back.

The mental toughness gained from persevering in these experiences will help them in all aspects of life. This includes helping them to be better at sports and other activities. The accomplishment and the feeling of success that come from the successful completion of these types of challenges builds self-esteem in a very solid and personal way.

Scouting is not a checklist. Anyone who runs through it checking everything off without getting the pickling brine on them will get little in return. Many young men pass through without ever testing themselves by facing these types of experiences. Many parents want to drop them off at camp, late the night before and pick them up in the morning. While they do get to check off a night at camp, they miss the character-building, life-changing opportunities that these types of experiences provide. They miss the essence of Scouting. They miss the bike ride in the sun.

After years of challenging experiences, these young men will be mentally tough and able to overcome anything that life will place before them. This is how Scouting builds boys to men.

To quote Seth recently, "Scouting prepared me with mental toughness like nothing else I had experienced. I know that I can do tough stuff!"

Never quit. Never ever allow yourself to give up!

7 WHITE ROCK

I am one for thinking outside of the box. I like to teach the Scouts to improvise and make do with what they have.

As October rolled around, we continued our journey of hiking or biking for our camps. Great effort was being made to keep the boys physically active in all our activities. After all, a Scout takes an Oath to be Physically Fit. What better way to keep this promise than pretending to be a mule hiking up hills while strapped to a pack?

Our camps where becoming gradually more challenging and yet somehow easier. The Scouts were getting the basic skills down. So, it was time to throw them some planned curve balls. I call them privations.

A privation is a planned hardship or challenge. They are, by design, meant to stretch us, causing us to improve skills or search within ourselves. Many times, they will be effective at getting us to reach heavenward. They can be used to help the boys relate the known to the unknown. They are great tools to enhance learning, a vital part of working with youth. They help us create a purpose for our activities.

The Scouts planned an overnight camp to a location near what we refer to as White Rock in Perry, Utah. It is a large white out cropping in the face of a mountain that overlooks Willard Bay. It's a great location to catch some incredible sunset views, if you arrive before dark.

We parked and then I handed them their meal rations. Among them was a raw egg with the challenge to get it to camp without breaking it.

We set off up the hill to find this "White Rock". Though portions of the hike are quite steep, it was a short hike of only a mile and a half or so, yet it seemed so much further. We arrived just after dark. Our site was a great wooded spot, next to an ATV trail with a natural spring bubbling up.

Justin, one of the Scout dads was already on site with a blazing fire to guide us in. It was a welcomed sight in the cold darkness, but I was disappointed that the Scouts would not be able to struggle with building the campfire that night. Seeing them grind a block of magnesium into oblivion and then complain that it can't be done was becoming a tradition.

This was our coldest camp to date. It slipped below freezing and landed in the low 20's that night. Most of the Scouts had little experience and they were working on their Scoutcraft and the lower rank requirements. What better time to teach them how to make water safe to drink? It is one of the advancement requirements that needed to be completed.

I am a believer in the practical exercise. When it comes to Scout Craft Skills, I don't believe a lecture or classroom covers it. I love to see the Scouts use the skill in action, it helps them learn the value of the skill. Scouting is action, it is learning through doing. I believe that their struggles make them stronger and more resilient.

We finished setting up camp and then I launched one of my Scoutmaster surprises. The anticipation of what I might do causes them some degree of anxiety and excitement.

During their menu planning, they agreed to have me bring an unknown element, a Scoutmaster surprise if you will, for dinner. When the time arrived to cook dinner, I handed each of them an onion and a hunk of raw hamburger. I demonstrated how to make a mini Dutch oven out of the onion and cook the burger. These went well and, let me say, ooh! If you ever want a juicy tasty burger this is the way to go. Just add a dash of steak seasoning and the result is mouthwatering!

We had some weeping and some excitement. Some struggled with the idea of cooking our food in the fire. Remember, just a few outings back we had to overcome the aversion to cooking on the fire. Now, right into the fire, we placed our onions and burgers, our little Dutch ovens and waited. Some were successful, some not so much.

Patience is a virtue that is earned as it is experienced.

Of course, my darker side found entertainment in the reaction of those Scouts who had never eaten a hamburger outside of its native form, meaning a patty on a bun. Some were grossed out. Some were afraid of the burger cooked in the onion. Others were more adventurous. All seemed to benefit from the experience of trying something new – eliminating needless fears and gaining experience in preparing their own food.

The Scouts love to ask me if their food is done. My patented response is always, "I don't know. It depends on how you like it." I continue to refuse to tell them when their food is done. Providing the answers seems to be counterintuitive to learning. They, the Scouts, like us, want the answers without ever having to pay the price to know. I feel that knowledge is best retained when it is experienced. Besides, taste is an individual preference.

Sometimes they burn their food, sometimes it is undercooked. Either way, they get to experience the results of their own efforts. One of my roles in working with youth is to aid them or set up opportunities for them to gain experience, make choices, and to own up to them. It requires a great deal of restraint, at times, to accomplish this. It is far, far easier to just prepare their food, or do it all for them, than to watch it play out and help with the aftermath.

Following a good night's sleep on the frozen ground, we arose to make our hot cocoa and prepare breakfast. Doing so required that they collect water and make it safe for drinking.

It was at this moment that I may have let slip that the puddle of water was deer pee. It just seemed to add a sense of urgency to getting the water sterilized correctly. Later, I had to quickly explain myself to at least one mom, as I overheard her son tell her that we drank deer pee. Oh man, Moms, please forgive me.

For the second Scoutmaster surprise, I handed each Scout an orange to go with their egg. The new challenge was to cook the egg in the orange, after you eat the center out.

Having done this before, I warned the Scouts to cook it fast and to not allow the egg to linger in the orange rind. Some, listened, and some experienced the tart flavor of an egg infused with the flavor of burnt orange rind. Burnt-orange-flavored egg is not at the top of the list of favorite foods – not on anyone's.

The broken eggs were the catalyst for the next round of venting frustrations that took place. Some of the Scouts were mortified that their egg was broken.

To quote, "I can't eat my egg!"

My response, "Why?"

"Because it has shell in it!" yelled a Scout, as if shell was some form of poison or contamination.

My reply, "So, eggshell is good for you and it's a good source of calcium."

"But I broke it and now its ruined because the shell is mixed in," said another Scout.

I went on to explain that it was okay to eat the egg with pieces of shell, it was just calcium. So, we cleaned it up as best we could, cooked and ate it. Later, we enjoyed some oatmeal, the backup breakfast.

I would never really let a Scout starve. I just don't want them to know that.

You truly get to know people as you spend time with them. Add a little adversity or privations to the mix and you both will receive a revelation as to who they really are. Our true selves come to the surface when the grind is on. How we behave under duress is very telling of our character.

Challenging experiences work to knock some of our rough edges off. The privations shape us into something more. Privations are to our spiritual and emotional well-being, what cardio and weight training are to our physical well-being. They point us towards our potential. They, by their nature, stretch us and we become stronger as a result.

This is Scouting, to gain experience, to learn to lead and to solve problems. Like a rainbow after the rain, self-esteem and well-being are the natural result of passing through challenging experiences.

After all of the complaining and venting of frustrations, they seem to remember and even brag, about conquering the adverse challenges.

8 GIVING YOUR BEST
Why do we do 50 miler bike rides or 50 miles hikes or even mile swims in cold lakes?

It is doing these types of challenges that brings many character flaws and strengths to bear. This is a great challenge for most of us, but an exceptional challenge to the younger and less athletic Scouts. Many of whom did not have the best gear to ride or experience.

Our troop ride was a challenge, requiring several pit repairs along the way, but they made it. They rode the 50 miles in under 8 hours and they discovered that they CAN!

I believe in coaching them to discover themselves, which leads to greater success. My old football coach would say to us during practice, "give me one more." While we were doing pushups, "just give me one more." He would repeat this getting you to give him one more until you had given him maybe fifty more, one at a time. The scene plays out much like the coach and Broc, the football captain in the movie "Facing the Giants". The scene takes place on the football field. The team is having a practice session. Broc claims that he was giving his best, that he couldn't do any more.

The coach then asks Broc if he has already written off Friday night's game, because he already knows they are going to lose.

The coach next challenged him to do the Death Crawl for 50 yards with another player on his back. Broc does not believe that he can crawl the 50 yards, but he is willing to try.

He blind folded Broc and told him to give his best. He repeated the challenge to him, to give his best, his absolute best. Broc then agrees to do his best.

Broc begins his crawl.

As Broc is crawling he yells "I can't!"

The coach responds, "You can!"

Broc yells back, "It's too hard"

The coach responds, "No, it is not! You keep going! You owe me your best!"

As the coach sees Broc struggle at the ¾ point, he tells him, "It's all heart from here, just give me your best. Give me everything you've got! When you have given your best, there shouldn't be anything left."

Broc yells that, "it is difficult, it's hard!"

The coach responds with, "give me five more, give me five more," meaning, give me five more yards. "You keep going" the coach is going right alongside him and becomes ever more intense, "give me five more, give me one more. You can!"

Broc crawls the full length of the football and into the end zone at the opposite end.

Broc collapses, complaining that it better be the 50-yard line because that's all he's got. He takes the blind fold off and he sees that he is in the end zone. He never thought he could do the 50 yards, and now without even realizing it, he has just crawled into the end zone. 100 yards!

We deceive ourselves when we decide that we can't before we even start. I see this so many times with parents in our current society. And it will be the same with our sons, unless we create opportunities to influence them in ways that show them that they can. They can ride or hike 50 miles, they can do hard things. *They are capable of so much more than they know, than we expect.* We can do better and so can they.

Our role, like that of the coach, is to help them discover this truth for themselves. Many are never shown what they can accomplish, and they settle for much less. Electronics and society are exasperating the problems. We are cuddling when we should be inspiring and motivating.

All these young men are capable of soaring to greatness. Coach them to make it, inspire them.

During our troop's 50-mile bike ride I found myself saying "Just a little further," and "Give me one more mile," and "You can do it!" repeated numerous times with numerous Scouts. They need to do their thing, but so do we as coaches, parents and mentors. We have a responsibility to not accept the half-shod attempt, but to inspire them to excel and to complete what they start. Our role is to help them identify and to see the higher target.

Pushing Through

Written somewhere among my personal tenets is never accept their desire to quit; never let them give up. This is NOT really what they want. It may be what they say, but they do want to win, they want to achieve. Sometimes they just need someone to show them what that looks like.

Inspire them to the finish line. Sometimes all they need is to know that you are there.

A fifty miler in the hot sun, uphill and with the wind in your face, is a great opportunity to meet this need. Doing and accomplishing is where true self-esteem, self-worth comes from.

If you want to see them stand a little taller, feel more confident and respect themselves and others a little more, help them to accomplish tough stuff. Teach them to serve and do because it is the right thing to do.

When we couple these physical and mental challenges with service to others, the positive effects upon our young sons are explosive!

Pulling them along by leading out, because they don't like to be pushed, and helping them to accomplish and complete challenging tasks, is where the forge to manhood lies. The very secret to a successful man is in unlocking the 'work ethic'. Show me a boy who possesses it and I will show you a man who can accomplish – anything.

One of the sweetest things ever said to me by one of the Scouts is: "I knew I couldn't do it, until I did it."

Or this one: "Scouting has affected my life by helping me with mental toughness."

Tyler, one of my Scouts, tried to insult me in front of his mom. It ended up being a great compliment. To quote Tyler, "I hate your Scouting because you make me do stuff (hike, food drives, fires, camp, etc.). "

Though Tyler stated that he hated it, he loved it and of course went on to become an Eagle Scout.

Imagine the determination of a young man who has passed through these experiences and many more. Imagine his ability to lead and to motivate others. His confidence and abilities will have been born from the school of experience. His heart will burn with the passion of overcoming adversity and he will know how sweet the taste of victory is.

A motivated and determined man will be a successful man!

9 BREAKFAST IS IN THE BAG

One of the things I choose to NOT accept from the Scouts is the phrase, "I can't." Whenever I hear those words, I will immediately dig in to help him know that HE CAN!

Experience is a true teacher. Looking back at some of the camps from my youth, I recall arriving late on one occasion and we had to locate our campsite and set up in the pitch black. It was a camp located in a wooded area that we were unfamiliar with. To make it more challenging, we had forgotten our flashlights. It was pitch black that night and we had to feel our way along the trail to our campsite. Some of the Scouts were using the matches to read the trail head signs along the way. As my cousin stated, it was like reading brail. My dad, the Scoutmaster, was busting us pretty good. He chided continuously, "What kind of troop is this anyway?"

"Why don't you live the Scout Motto?"

"Why aren't you prepared?"

"How are you Scouts going to find your camp?"

I never thought, at the time to quip back to him, that we were the kind of troop that he trained. I did, however, take note that as he pressed us for not having our flashlights and spare matches, that he didn't have any with himself either.

On another occasion, my cousin Jim and one of the Clark boys found a spot that was already cleared for their tent. It was smooth and free of vegetation. The ground was soft. My dad, our Scoutmaster at the time, suggested to them that it was a bad idea to pitch their tent in the gulley. They replied about how it was perfect, their tent nestled so nicely into place. They knew that they had the perfect spot and there was no persuading them otherwise.

Later, another troop from Richmond, Indiana joined us. As evening progressed this troop complained that all they had brought with them were two pieces of plastic. Jimmie, my cousin, and Dean Clark had noticed some rain clouds gathering, so they negotiated with this unsuspecting troop and swapped their tent for the plastic. The boys from Richmond were ecstatic that they would get to sleep in the tent.

Jim and Dean set up on the high ground with the plastic stretched between two trees and some rocks for weight.

My dad had been observing the tent placement and the negotiations. He issued the same warning to the Richmond Scouts. They were too content with their new digs to care.

Knowing it was a bad idea, he let them do it anyway. He knew that experience was the better teacher in this case.

Later that night, at about 1 am, the rain let loose with a famous midwestern down pour. Within a few minutes, the gulley where they had pitched their tent had water running through it like a small river. The tent, being open to the high side, made a perfect funnel and they were soaked in no time at all. I observed their tent go down the gulley like a fat man riding a slip-n-slide. Some of the Scouts were still inside as it made its way down. They spent the remainder of the night around the fire trying to get dry and warm.

The next morning, some of the camp officials made their way around the campsites. Jim and Dean received recognition for being the only dry Scouts. We still have some good laughs about the experience. I do feel bad for the Scouts in the tent, but I had no part in their negotiations and both parties thought that they were taking advantage of the other, which led them into making the poor choice.

Flash back to the present. For our next adventure as Troop #210, we went to Willard Bay. The night almost passed without an incident as the Scouts were now growing accustomed to cooking their own food, setting up camp, and dealing with whatever mess they made.

The first highlight came as I looked over my shoulder and noticed Adam dancing a jiggity-jig and trying to lift both of his feet unsuccessfully off the ground at the same time. I rushed over and began to assess the situation. I could tell there was something up with his feet, so I took him to the ground. Adam then began to explain the situation and what he had done. I was quickly taken back to some things that he had been saying over the summer.

He had seen it on YouTube that you can walk on hot coals if you set your mind to it. He had been set on attempting this. After all, if it's on the internet, it must be true.

Despite our earlier warnings, he was convinced that YouTube knew best. On this night without warning, and when no one was looking, he had removed his shoes and attempted to walk on our campfire. I say attempted because he was the immediate recipient of the consequences of his choice and had to abort. The grand master of instructors had struck again, this time in our troop.

He now had 1st and 2nd degree burns that were coal shaped on the pads of his feet. They were square and angular, just like the grains in a glowing coal. I sat him down on the ground and began to render aid. As I did so, his father looked at me and said, "Why did you let him do that?" To which, I quickly responded, "No, why did YOU let him do that?"

At this moment, I was grateful to have not only a parent with us, but more importantly, his parent. To add to my relief, he was a doctor.

The various burns were small to severe in their nature. Both of his feet were burned in the mid foot area (very tender) and on the pads.

Young bodies regenerate and recover ever so quickly. Adam was no exception and he recovered without any permanent damage (thankfully). Adam, like the Scouts, from the Richmond troop, has now been schooled in an indelible way by the dean of experience. This is something that we all fall prey to when we are unable to accept wisdom and reason from the experience of others. He now had firsthand knowledge that regardless of YouTube, fire and coals will burn you.

The next morning it was time to launch the next Scoutmaster surprise. As we began to setup for breakfast, I handed out paper bags, two eggs and 2 strips of bacon to each Scout. I gave them instructions and demonstrated how to accomplish the task at hand, using the E.D.G.E. method. This was again a game of technique and patience. I had first seen this method of cooking years ago when I was a Scout.

Look back with me to the 1970's when my dad served as our troop's Scoutmaster for a period. Though he was never trained in the Scouting ways, he held our attention. He was a sort of MacGyver who could solve any problem that he would encounter using whatever was in his proximity.

One fall weekend, we found ourselves on a district camp out in the Dayton, Ohio area. In the morning, he issued a challenge that whoever prepared their breakfast with the least amount of clean up needed afterwards would get donuts added to their menu. Only one winner would be awarded. Having one winner motivated us to compete, to do our best, everyone wanted those donuts.

We all began scheming how to cook with the bare minimum of utensils being involved. I was feeling pretty good at the thought of mixing and cooking with the same metal bowl and using only a fork.

And then he did it. Dad used the tripod that had been set up over the fire. I was in disbelief that what he was about to attempt could be done until I witnessed the results. He produced a paper bag and cooked two eggs with bacon in the bag. When the eggs were fully cooked, he peeled the bag down and ate them right out of it. Then, he tossed the bag into the fire and had absolutely nothing left to clean up. What a genius idea. At that moment I was both frustrated and jealous.

We studied how it was that the bag didn't burn up when hanging over the fire. Soon, we were cooking in paper cups and other items to show off our newfound knowledge of how liquid keeps the cup, or bag, from igniting. It felt good to come to this conclusion through our own experimentation.

And now after waiting over 40 years, it was my opportunity to use this technique on some Scouts or otherwise unsuspecting persons.

Each of the Scouts in Troop #210 met the task with varied success. Some of the Scouts are more vigilant and others have more patience. Some attempted to rush through the exercise and failed in the process. Cooking in a paper bag is one of those things in life that simply cannot be rushed. It is a slow cooking process that requires time. Time, even minutes, can seem to be an eternity to a hungry 12-year-old.

While the more patient Scouts in Troop #210 enjoyed the benefits of a yummy breakfast and nothing to cleanup, others were left to develop more patience and find something else to eat.

It is a difficult thing to allow them to fail. There are times when the best thing we can do as parents or leaders is to watch from a distance and allow them to fail. To fail is to create a fertile planting bed for learning and discovery. We can then encourage them to give it another try, and then another, until they achieve the goal. Eventually, they learn that persistence has its reward. A new skill once mastered will not likely be forgotten. Effort and perseverance pay off in the end.

Helping them to learn this process, is key to their future success and something that I enjoy passing down to them.

Cooking in a paper bag over a fire requires a good deal of patience. The bag needs to be in proximity to the heat to cook and yet far enough from the flame that it doesn't ignite. Some just never seem to have enough patience to see it through. They want an immediate result.

When they push for it, the usual immediate result is a torched breakfast.

Performing service projects as part of our camps had become a troop tradition. This camp was no exception as we volunteered to do a conservation project for the park ranger.

We went to work clearing the way for a new trail, bridge, and observation area to be built. We trimmed, pruned, and hauled. Some of us did battle with a few thorns and received some battle scars that were like trophies to the Scouts.

The Scouts worked hard; the harder we went at it, the more effort they put into it, the more they seemed to be having a good go of it, having fun. They were smiling and egging each other on. They were pushing us, the leaders, as well. I was loving it. I wondered what was driving this.

At the conclusion of the camp, we held a reflection, a powerful tool for reinforcing learning, that I have been working on mastering. I can hear vividly, Kaleb, telling me that he loved this camp. As I asked what his favorite part was, he stated, "The service project!"

"Why?" I asked.

He said, "because it was fun doing it and it made me feel like I made a difference. We accomplished something today that will help others!"

Hmm... that what they did mattered. I thought to myself, wow! This struck me as powerful, even more so coming from this young man. I was again learning from them.

Consider that this insight was found while working on a service project, not while playing video games, not while doing sports, not in a comfortable chair, it was brought to bear while in the service of others. Service is such an unlikely place for a young man to find joy. Or is it?

This thought, his comment, was enlightening to me. Instead of telling me that he can't or won't or even that he would rather do something else or anything else, this Scout was telling me that he would rather help someone, that he wanted to make a difference. Really?

As we continued our reflection, his words sank into my heart. The other Scouts were telling me something similar.

I often hear people say, that they can't get boys to help or do things that they are asked. Does letting them be in charge make the difference? Maybe, some of them have never been shown or given the opportunity, to lead or to engage in service to others.

I learned from those young men. I learned that they want to matter. They want to make a difference. They are naturally wired to work and to do for others. Self-worth and character emerge when we engage in these types of activities. Those Scouts love the idea of contributing. They love to serve others and the feeling of accomplishment. Sometimes, they just need a little nudge, to help them discover this truth.

Good things happen when we follow inner promptings.

Boys learn by imitating what they see. This can be dangerous and sometimes their desire to do gets warped when all they have been shown is the movie or video version of life. Worse yet, some young men do not have good role models in their life. And they will to a good degree follow what models they do have, including the undesirable.

Movies and wealth often teach that joy can only be found in gifts and entertainment. This is a false assumption.

Our youth need, us, to step up. Mentoring these youth to strengthen their families and their faith in GOD is one of the greatest opportunities and responsibilities that rest upon us.

A SCOUT IS

Trustworthy, Loyal, Helpful, Friendly, Courteous, Kind, Obedient, Cheerful, Thrifty, Brave, Clean and Reverent.

These simple words can have such a powerful and lasting effect on one's life.

It takes about 4 years of repeating the Scout Law before it becomes permanently set in the mind. That's one reason why you can't become an Eagle and get the full benefit of Scouting in two years. True Scouting, like most successes in life cannot be accomplished by merely completing a checklist. One must get pickled in the brine, so to speak. When we cheat the time, we don't achieve the desired result and the Scout Oath and Scout Law will fade from memory and not have the lasting effect that they were meant to have.

Once set in, those words will be carried in the mind and heart of the beholder and become a moral code of conduct for them, throughout their lifetimes.

10 WINTER CAMP -LEGRAND'S GRAVEL PIT

I camped in the snow and ice once while my boys were growing up. I was volunteered as a dad, to accompany my son's Scout troop up Cottonwood Canyon. I was told that it was no big deal, that I just needed to come. I was not given any special equipment list or instructions for this camp. So off we went. I had no idea, what lie ahead for this outing.

It turned out to be the longest and coldest night of my life, ever. I vowed never to be that dumb again.

I lay awake freezing most of the night during that camp. That morning, I arose chilled to the bone and we had no means of making a fire to warm ourselves.

The previous night, we had a fire barrel that we left burning as we went to sleep. By morning, it had melted through enough ice to sink, what seemed to me about six feet or so down. Unless we were looking to hire a rabbit to retrieve it, there was not going to be a fire. It was now refrozen down that hole and it would remain there, until the snow melted sometime in the coming summer.

The night before, I was instructed to make a ditch for sleeping and lay in it. The second option offered was that I could join the boys in a snow cave. Being claustrophobic, this really left me with only one choice. So, I made my ditch, laid my tarp down and slid into my sleeping bag. I laid there with uncontrollable shivering and gnashing of my teeth all through the night. I was experiencing hypothermia.

By morning, I was exhausted and chilled through to the bone. I could not stop shivering. My bones ached, my body was stiff, and I was moving slowly. I was wondering why the hell anyone would ever do this. What was the point? I was feeling miserable at this moment.

Fast forward a few years and I am now a Scoutmaster. Here, I am now prepping to camp, once more, in the snow, ice, and artic cold of the northern Utah winters. What was I thinking? How could I even entertain the idea of becoming involved in a winter camp? Then, again as Scoutmaster, how could I not be involved? I'm now the one who was supposed to have 'mastered' the Scout craft, right?

I knew that I could not lead these boys if I was not willing to do the camp with them and show them how easy it was. I was also sure that I did not want anyone to have the experience that I had, camping with my son's troop. It had been a miserable experience that I did not care to repeat.

I noted that this is one more of the many items in a long list that they had conveniently left off the job description when they were roping me into becoming a Scoutmaster.

I knew, from experience, that you will freeze if you have any air movement over you. I also knew that you had to have some insulation between you and the ground. Though I was going on this great freezeout, I was not going to give experience, the master teacher, the opportunity to repeat my earlier lessons. I had learned indelible lessons from my son's camp out and did not want to repeat them.

Kevin, the assistant Scoutmaster, assured me this time would be different because we were camping on "insulated concrete blankets." I bought into the theory and away we went into the freezing cold to brave another night in hopes that it would be better.

With the previous experiences accounted for in our preparations, our camp went without a hitch.

It worked. We had no frozen casualties. "Be Prepared" makes the difference!

As a highlight during this outing, the boys discovered, or at least adapted, a recipe to be their own. Dutch oven Scoutmaster pie was born. It was the Scouts' version of shepherd's pie. They used tater tots, green beans, gravy, and a few other camp ingredients, and I watched as the Scouts ate it up. I witnessed that eating their concoction was some form of trophy to them. How was that? They ate green beans, really? They never eat green beans. They had prepped it. They had cooked it. They had served it up and they ate it all. Or maybe, it was because there really wasn't anything else to eat. This could be useful for future outings, I thought to myself.

Then it was off to go ice fishing.

This was my last camp with Troop #210 and surprisingly, there were no unusual occurrences. At least that's how I remember it. Everything went smoothly and as planned. The boys had a grand time ice fishing with the old timers. Judging from the laughter, I'd say the old timers had some fun sharing their ice fishing expertise with the Scouts. It was heartwarming to see the connection between them.

Our time together as Troop #210 ended. Now, as I look back, I think they enjoyed the mutual experiences, not because we went anywhere or did anything exotic, rather simply because we went, and we did. They knew that they mattered to us and to everyone that we touched through service. We were moving! We never failed to go with the Scouts or to carry out our planned activities. They knew we were dependable. Nothing stopped us, not rain, not snow, not heat, not even the subzero weather! We were living the example that we expected from them.

I left Troop #210 with more knowledge, skills, and certainly a much better attitude than when I had arrived. I am grateful for the experiences and the memories. I, too, was changed by the experiences that we shared.

I will cherish the time and the adventures. More importantly, I saw the changes and growth in each of the boys and the leaders that were involved. From this group, Seth, Jeremy, Adam and Wiley are all Eagles, and they are already doing great things with their lives.

Scouting made a difference in their lives. Now they are using their lives to make a difference!

IF WE DID EVERYTHING THAT WE WERE CAPABLE OF DOING, WE WOULD LITERALLY ASTONISH OURSELVES

AUTHOR UNKNOWN

11 SURVIVING CANADA
The experiences of a fourteen-year-old Scout.
The Seal River Expedition

Okay, so maybe this one shouldn't be included in a motivational book, but it is one of my own real experiences. I am including it as it gives a glimpse into my background, of the experiences that influence my work with these young men. I was fourteen years old. This true-life event gives us a window view of what a 14-year-old is capable of.

To set the stage, once we left the system of lakes leading us to the river, we never encountered another human being, until we emerged at the other end, after having traveled some 450 miles. The remote area of the Seal River is subarctic and lies in the northern region of Manitoba Canada.

In August of 1978, I accompanied a group of Scouts from the Dayton Ohio area and left to go canoeing on the Seal River through Manitoba Canada. We traveled up through the Dakotas. We drove out to a remote logging area, with little of anything else around. When we parked, our leaders took the batteries and valuables from the vehicles and buried them, in hopes that they would be there when we returned.

We launched our canoes, lashed together side by side, onto the system of lakes that would eventually lead us to the Seal River. Our leader, Woodford, had a small engine that he used to tow the six canoes as we began our journey into the unknown. The progress was painfully slow, but hey it was better than paddling across the seemingly endless lake.

Eventually, a group of native Canadians spotted us. They first had to show off the power of their boat by speeding around us a few times. Finally, they approached and offered to be our tug for a fee, of course. This was welcomed assistance as we were getting nowhere fast.

The trip in the beginning was going well and everyone's spirits were high. At this moment everything was new, we had plenty of supplies and food. The excitement of the adventure was intoxicating to us. We were anxious and willing to see what lay ahead for us.

We eventually made our way across the lake and around a glacier to a river that would take us to the Seal River. This first river gave us the opportunity to paddle against the current. It was slow going and to make it more challenging there were numerous log jams along the way. Most were satisfied by exiting their canoe and finding a way to portage around. I really didn't have the patience for that. For me, I was more interested in busting up those log jams, much like working a puzzle in reverse. When we approached the jams, I would exit out of the canoe and walk on the logs floating on the water. I would work one or two of them around looking for the key to the whole dam. There were usually one or two logs that were holding the rest of them up, creating the dam. If you nudged the right ones, the group would begin to break apart and a path would open for us to continue making our way against the current.

The group must have approved of my efforts, for in a short time I was placed in the lead canoe. They liked the idea that I kept things moving along. And I liked being the dam (log jam) buster.

The water was icy cold. And it became even colder once we entered the Seal River system.

We drank directly from the river. I suppose the cold temperature kept it safe for us to drink. Shrubs grew on the banks and into the flowing water, turning the water brown like tea. It had a taste to it, and it helped thinking of it as a watered-down tea.

The mosquitos were thick enough such that if you did not use your mosquito netting, you would breath them in. After a time, you grew accustomed to having to look through them to see through your mosquito netting.

One of our stops along the way was a small Indian village. Their living was very meager and primitive by our standards. Their diet largely consisted of what their hunting and fishing skills would bring them and little else. They taught us to make Bannock or skillet bread. A simple recipe that required so few ingredients that even a Scout could make it.

They had an Eagle that we were able to handle and interact with. He would come close enough that you could appreciate the size of his talons and the strength of his beak as he would tear the flesh of his dinner apart.

They had a few items for which I was grateful including a canvas cabin tent with a woodstove on one end. This warm tent was one of the most welcomed luxuries at this point in the trip.

They helped us fish and they gave us some flour to make more Bannock. While there one of the ladies made me a pair of smoked-moose-hide mittens. I left her with $5.

Their vocabulary was one that would make any sailor blush. Their shotguns used almost daily for hunting, a necessity if you wanted to eat, were mostly broken and in disrepair. I do not believe any of them had a butt stock.

One oddity that I witnessed was seeing them make a slit around the shot shell so that it would be expelled like a slug.

We left the family and continued our journey. They imparted to us some knowledge of the local landscape and some much-needed navigational tips. The days went quickly by. Time was slipping away as we continued our journey. I am sure our leaders knew, but did not share with us, that we were behind schedule. Some of the connecting waters that we used may or may not have been the correct ones. But whatever the issues were, we were behind schedule, colder weather was coming, and of course our food supply was getting thin.

To prepare for this trip we had to meet certain requirements. Among those requirements was to complete the swimming merit badge. One of the requirements was to jump into deep water, fully dressed, shoes and all, and while treading water, remove your clothes and turn them into a floatation device. Another requirement was to make our own rucksack. No framed packs were allowed on this trip. All our personal gear plus our food had to fit into the pack. We were limited on space and of course weight.

We had the bare necessities with us. Pocket knife, mosquito net, rain suit, tent, sleeping bag, mess kit, spare socks, cup, hat, fishing pole, a sewing kit, and some dried food. I also carried along a journal.

Here is an excerpt from the actual journal that I kept:

"August 27, we are now two weeks out. We are beginning to get a little fatigued. Everyone is getting a little edgy, including Woodford, at times. There are all kinds of animal tracks here to follow including caribou, bear, and moose to name a few.

The mosquitos are awful. My food supply is getting low. I am worried about how to make it last.

My tent leaks and I am using plastic bags to keep dry, while in my tent, due to the incessant rain.

We leave our boots and socks on the fire at night, in hopes of drying them out before putting them back on the next day.

During one of the rapids yesterday, Larry Gonzales and Greg Garcia swamped their canoe and it stayed submerged as they paddled to shore. Larry lost his paddle and had to paddle with his hands to get to shore. We built a fire, dried them out and then continued our journey.

I can't wait until food is plentiful and good. I am looking forward to getting to Churchill so we can have a good meal.

Garcia had a dream last night that he was going to the restroom. And he did go while still asleep in his sleeping bag.

Food is low, no more extras or dressings – honey, jam, all gone.

As we were unloading our gear today, Bob threw his sleeping bag out of his canoe and onto the sloped riverbank. I watched helplessly as his bag rolled down and into the river. Now he is wondering if there was some form of foul play.

I paddled out this evening in my canoe to wash up and as I do, I observe the setting of the sun. The view is beautiful. The sun is shining for the first time in several days and reflecting off the water. I wonder at this moment just how incredible it is to be alive and to enjoy the outdoors and God's beautiful creations."

As our journey continued, eventually our leaders shared with us that we needed to be moving more and to somehow cover more mileage. We began to push the hours, cutting mealtimes, and fire time, which was important to get dry and warm. We also had to get out on the water earlier each day.

My tent was rotting from the dampness. This most likely started because I had put it away wet, from a previous camping trip. It was now being exasperated by the continuous dampness incurred during this trip. It seemed that we nor our gear were ever able to completely dry out. It was becoming covered in black mold and the zipper ripped out of my netting. I couldn't close the netting securely and the mosquitos and deer flies were eating me alive. It was miserable.

To deal with this development, I sewed one side of the tent opening completely shut and then I took a pair of my socks, cut them into strips and sewed them on as tabs, to tie the second side shut.

Our breakfast time was shortened. I no longer had time to cook my breakfast which up to this point had consisted of cream of wheat and hot cocoa. With the short time, I would just mix them together in my cup with hastily warmed water and then gulp it down. No cooking it until it was smooth and creamy. Some days I would just gulp it down raw and uncooked. For cleaning up I would just dangle the cup from a tether while we paddled on.

The longer workdays and food scarcity were having an effect upon us, in that we started to wear down physically, to the point of exhaustion. We pushed the limits on the rapids more, or at least it seemed to be so.

As we journeyed, we would portage around anything that looked too unpredictable, or that showed a class IV or above. Whitewater above a V was considered impossible.

With the weather changing, the water conditions were likewise changing and becoming increasingly unpredictable.

There were times that we had to port around the severe rapids. It was at those times that I was first to do my part in hoisting and carrying one of the canoes. Portaging meant carrying the 80 to 90-pound Grumman aluminum canoe on your shoulders and trekking over the rocky terrain.

It was common for at least one of the canoes to swamp on some of the more treacherous and challenging rapids. Mind you, that these rapids had waves that crashed over the canoes and rocks that would destroy one. They were swift and at times very narrow. Luckily, if one swamped, there were five other canoes to rescue you.

The water in the Seal River is icy cold, only the rapid movement keeps it from freezing.

The permafrost is an area of earth, that never gets above 32 degrees. It remains frozen year-round or nearly year-round. We were there. The area in northern Manitoba is considered sub-arctic. By the end of the trip, we also had firsthand experience of the Tundra, an area of earth where it just becomes too cold for anything to grow.

Eventually, we ran into a spell of bad weather. It was severe enough that we had to hole up in our tents for two days. Wind, heavy rain, and hail stones kept us company through the night. On the day we emerged it was freezing cold, even icy.

There was no one to rescue us, no one to build a warm fire, or offer dry clothes. If we wanted to be warm, we had to build it. We became frugal and anticipative of our resources.

One of the highlights of being so far north, was the ability to see the northern lights. They are magical. It was fun to witness their ghostly glows in the sky.

We had in our company 13 souls. One was a Scout who seemed to be wimpy. He enjoyed being the third man in the canoe. He was just more content to not have to work. He complained a lot and did not like doing his share of the work. His last name was Garcia.

One day, as fate would have it, Garcia was assigned to ride with Woodford, our leader. The river was wide at this section. There were plenty of white caps and strong currents to provide plenty of challenges navigating and staying upright. The rapids on this day seemed to take us by surprise and so we were not fully prepared to navigate the intense violence of them.

For the more challenging rapids we would usually paddle to the banks of the river and exit the canoes to form a plan of attack for successfully navigating the rapids. This would include surveying the conditions of the river, the obstacles, and hazards and how best to work them.

Maybe, the pressure of running behind schedule, the weather or the fact that we were running out of food drove us a little longer. Maybe, someone decided to push it too far. I will never know.

What happened next was life changing. We swamped our canoes. I was thrown out into the icy waters of the Seal River. My rain suit was of little help at this moment as my body felt the shock of the cold water. And I had to fight my survival instincts to thwart off panicking.

I felt skilled in navigating and maintaining a low center of gravity, while in the canoe. I can handle the canoe safely under most circumstances. Up to this point, along with many of our crew, I had never been ejected from my canoe, no matter how violent the water had been. But on this day the rapids took most of us out. I was ejected from our canoe so quickly, that I can't recall exactly what happened or why. My legs were tangled in a rope tethered from the canoe preventing me from swimming. I had to free myself quickly while flowing down river in the rapids.

Everyone had swamped to varying degrees on that day except the canoe with Garcia and Woodford. Though they had taken on water, they were able to quickly get to shore, and relaunch. The fact that they did not swamp on that day saved our lives! Each of us were in peril of either drowning or suffering hypothermia at that moment and most of us likely would not have survived.

Hypothermia is a medical emergency that occurs when your body loses heat faster than it can produce heat, causing a dangerously low body temperature. The signs and symptoms of hypothermia are: First: shivering, reduced circulation; Second: slow, weak pulse, slowed breathing, lack of co-ordination, irritability, confusion and sleepy behavior; Advanced: slow, weak or absent respiration and pulse. Death follows.

Survival time in 32-degree water – less than 15 minutes due to exhaustion and unconsciousness. Attempting to swim accelerates the heat loss and exhaustion.

Death occurs is less than 45 minutes.

I believe that at least seven or eight of the thirteen of us, had been ejected when our canoes swamped from the violence of the rapids. Carter was stranded with his canoe wrapped around a rock. I saw him as I floated by being carried downstream. It was breached around a boulder and he was trying frantically to remove it, to save it and himself.

For me, I began to swim to the left shore. It looked to be the closest. I was fighting off the temptation to panic and giving it everything that I had in my attempt to swim. I was exerting everything left in me to get to the shore. It seemed as if the land was passing me by in fast motion. I was going down river. And I was going fast. I was powerless against the swift current that seemed to have gripped me. My struggle seemed to be in vain, as I could not realize any progression towards the riverbank.

At some point, Garcia and Woodford paddled to me. They had some others in their canoe. I was already too cold to do much at that point. I was having difficulty moving. They somehow managed to get me to hold onto the side of the canoe. It was all that could be done. I was shivering, cold and weak. They seemed to be rushing. I exerted all the strength in my hands to hold on. It was all I or they could do.

For a moment, I was angry: I had been swimming to the left and they were taking me to the right. Why, I thought, I need to go to shore? They were taking me back out. I was feeling some panic at the thought.

They paddled me over to a small island in the middle of the river. It was all rock. Garcia helped me to get out of the water as I was too cold to move on my own.

What was happening. Oh, leave me alone. I thought to myself. I just want to sleep now. I curled up on the rock, barely out of the water. I needed to sleep. Just let me sleep. I felt nothing else at that moment.

They left me as they went to rescue others that were still in the water. I was unaware of anything else until they came back for me. I was being smacked in the face and someone was shaking me. They were yelling my name. What, why are you doing this? I thought. They loaded me back into a canoe and took me to land. Someone had started a fire. A big fire.

I was stripped down and placed in a dry bag next to the fire. In a short time, they were pouring hot liquids down me.

Next, I saw them working on Jammie and Tim. They seemed to be worse off. They were stripped and placed in sleeping bags with others. They were slurring their speech and they were attempting to crawl into the fire. They seemed to be delirious. Someone had to watch them and pull them back.

The world seemed to be racing by. I was somehow in slow motion, why was everything going so fast it all seemed to be blurry? Please, slow down. I can't keep up. Wait, what are you saying? You are talking too fast.

Some time had passed before I began to understand what had transpired. Most of our group had swamped. All of us were at least soaked. Several of us had lost our canoes, except Garcia. AND he had somehow become a hero. He and Woodford had somehow saved us all.

Carter's canoe was on shore now. A crew was jumping up and down in it, attempting to flatten it enough for us to use it again. It had a reverse arch to it.

Some from our group were off searching for and rescuing our gear. Nothing much was said about what had just happened. The talk was now all about piecing together what we had so that we could continue. We assessed what we had left, as there would be no help, and there was no way to get word out for help. The only way out was to see this journey through to the end. The way out, and the only way out was to finish it, to make it to the end.

For you young folks, you must realize that we were truly on our own. There were no cell phones or GPS units, no trackers. Even if they existed, they would not have worked in this remote area. The fly overs for search and rescue are rare because no one is in these remote areas to look for.

Without divine intervention, all our gear would have been gone. Even if we could have made it out of the water, we would have been wet, and freezing with no food or supplies or shelter. If that one canoe had not made it out of the water, all of us would not have survived. There is no question about it. If Garcia had not grown a heart and stepped up, all of us would not have survived. Was God's hand in this? I believe so. I believe that what happened was exactly what each of us needed. Garcia was changed in that moment. He went from being a zero to a hero!

The best Scouting experiences are the near-death ones. Because they cause us to recognize and to call upon HIM. We learn more about who we are in these moments under these circumstances. Look at Garcia, this complaining, pain-in-the-butt kid. Suddenly, he is a hero and grows six inches in stature that day. His self-esteem grew ten-fold in that very moment. We suddenly became friends bound by a common traumatic event.

Pushing Through

I would never hazard a Scout to this extreme. However, if I could give every Scout this same type of experience, with the same outcome, I would do it today without hesitation.

As we regrouped and assessed our situation, we recovered all the canoes. Carter's canoe, though it was severely damaged, was rendered usable again. We had tents and sleeping bags. Some things were soaked but mostly recovered. The most important loss was that we went from having an extra paddle to being short one.

The decision was made to make one. We cut down a pine tree. Trying to find one small enough to manipulate and to work it with our knives, and yet large enough to have a cross section big enough to make a paddle was a challenge. Gonzales was the engineer of the project.

We took turns using our makeshift paddle. As most complained about using it, I happily volunteered to use the tree. My arms grew rapidly weary with the weight of it and the splash, splash, splash. It really wasn't much of a paddle at all. The pilot in the stern of the canoe had to do most of the work to compensate.

In a short time, I was holding that piece of sap-soaked wood next to my torso and using a twisting motion with my body to row. It was heavy and it seemed to be gaining weight. There was no issue holding on to it though as the sap made a great grip glue.

As days passed, we were running out of food. We were relying heavily on catching fish daily. We began to follow bear scat when on land. The scat would get more frequent and point like a funnel towards a food source. We learned to follow it to berries. If the bears had been eating them, then they must be safe for us to eat. We ate all that we could find.

On one evening, as we were working to find something to eat, Carter was fishing. He had been working the river and caught a fish. It looked like a nice size northern Pike. As we watched him, we were imagining what that fish was going to taste like.

He worked it and in that same moment that he brought it to shore, a bear ran out of the brush, next to us and snagged that fish from him.

In that same moment we were instantly angry and began to chase the bear down. As we yelled and pursued, we also, in an instant realized, that hey it's a bear! We let him have it, of course.

A few days or a day later. I broke my fishing line and lost my Canadian swivel in the mouth of a Northern Pike. You know, as do I, that, it would have been the biggest one that you ever saw. But it got away. I was left without dinner, the only real meal of the day.

Feeling down and hungry. I saw Barret had an angle on one that he was working. He brought it ashore and it was a beauty. It was at least thirty inches long. Those fillets would feed most of us very well.

We went to tend to other duties and build the fire up in preparation to cook the fish.

When we returned to Barret and his fish, we inquired where it was. He had a nice fillet in his mess kit all prepped to cook.

He answered, "I threw it in the river." "What?" was our reply. He continued saying that he took what he wanted, figuring that no one needed it, and tossed the rest of it or rather most of it into the river.

We were ready to take him and toss him into the river, because at that moment no one wanted Barret, only his fish.

Another story about Barret. He was a tall and slender built lad, with red hair. He spoke with a southern drawl and slowly.

One day, we were all gathered around the evening fire attempting to get dry and warm up. I was soaked from the day's events. And I was cold to the point of being numb. As we stood around the fire, I had my back turned and I was attempting to be as close as I could be to the fire. We did this at the day's end each day, it felt good to steam our pants dry.

I heard Barret's voice, speaking with his monotone drawl, very slowly and calm.

"Hey, Paul," slight pause, "Ug, I think (pause) your pants might be on fire." Of course, from the tone of his voice I found no reason to believe there was any urgency. As I causally turned to examine my pants, they were aflame and had burnt off to my knees. The back side of my pants was gone!

I, excitedly, responded to Barret that next time could he please yell to indicate the situation in a more urgent manner.

On one of our days, and it may have been the day we all swamped, Bruce, one of the adult leaders, had busted his shin bone. By busted I am referring to a broken shin bone. We know it was broken because it was bent out of shape. We applied our best Scout first aid, cutting strips of fabric from socks and tents, and using some sticks we applied a splint to it. At least he was able to be the odd man out and ride in the center of the canoe for a few days.

As we approached the end of our time on the river, we could no longer follow the flow of the river to find our way to the Hudson Bay. The tide was going out and the water was flowing in every direction possible. The sky was overcast and grey. We were in the tundra now, there were no more trees, there were no landmarks to be seen. Mostly mossy growth and a few shrubs as we approached the mouth of the Hudson Bay. There was very little land to be found.

On our last night before the Hudson, we made camp on some rocks, just high enough to keep us out of the water, which was flowing around us on all sides. There was no land. There wasn't a fire, because we didn't have any wood to make one with. We were in the tundra. We were so exhausted; we just wanted any place that we could get out of the canoes and be dry.

Floating around in the shallow but endless waters of the Delta, we struggled to find a piece of land large enough to afford us the opportunity.

After finding a place to tie off the canoes, we set up our tents. As we lay there in the dark eating the last of our soggy food scraps, a helicopter appeared overhead. It was a search and rescue unit. As we heard the thud from the rotor and saw the search light, I was thinking to myself and maybe even yelling it out loud, "We are saved!"

Oh, man, did we ever want that helicopter to land.

Our leaders refused the help. They agreed to having them get word, if possible, to our families that we were fine. None of us got a ride in the helicopter. There was simply an exchange of information and then they left.

Bruce's leg was by this time black and blue. He was moaning with pain and did not seem to be doing too well. With this thought in mind, I remember, saying, please – please let them at least take Bruce with them.

At that moment, I was as close to a mutiny as ever I have been. We were exhausted, our energy was depleted. Our emotions ran free and we doubted their decision at that moment. We, as Scouts, had difficulty understanding how they, the leaders, could not allow us to be rescued. We were not seeing an end to our current situation.

Now, years later, I am grateful that they waved them off. It was a wise choice. It is the one that I would make today. Rescuing us would have made us victims. Completing the adventure made us conquerors which makes all the difference.

A short time later we again found ourselves in over our heads as we entered the Hudson Bay. There was no possible way for us to traverse this massive body of water. At this time, I am not sure where they came from, but we found some native Canadians or rather they found us and made plans to tow us down the bay to Church Hill, Manitoba. In the notes included at the end of this chapter, there is travel information for the Seal River. The warning states the following about attempting to paddle the Hudson:

"Under no circumstances attempt the Hudson!"

We embarked on this leg of the journey to again within a short time, find ourselves in peril for our lives. All that could be seen in any direction was rolling water and a very grey sky. In no time the boats were being heaved up and then dropped on the rolling waves. The boat I was in was leaking from the stern and bottom of the hull. The pilot of the boat was fighting the waves with all she had. The engine was churning at its max. The stern was being ripped apart from the tug of our canoes being worked against the boat from the waves. The hull was flexing from being dropped on the water. The waves would pick the boats up and then drop them with enough force to flex the bottom of the hull. We were taking on water. To add to the excitement of the moment, the pilots were in a state of panic and expressing it so eloquently in the use of the vilest of words available in the English language.

One of our leaders, a test pilot from Wright Patterson Air Force Base was in my boat. He was so motion sick that he was laying curled up in a ball on the floor of the boat. He was being thrown upward with the waves and then slamming down hard on the floor of the boat. He was bouncing like a ball. He was so ill at the time that he was incapacitated and vomiting on himself.

There was little anyone could do except to hold on and to pray. The sky was grey and overcast. It was drizzling rain. We were cold, wet and just hoping to not be thrown overboard. I was certain that the boat was going to come apart at any moment. I was in a state of shock and feeling somewhat disconnected from the surreal scene that unfolding before my own eyes. Everyone was experiencing fear.

I was wondering what to do when it happened. How were we going to swim in these violent waves? Would anyone find us? I was mentally preparing for being ejected out into the cold, dark, ocean like waves. I was estimating how many clothes I would need to shed and what I would be able to hang onto once I was in the water. It didn't seem to be a matter of if, rather a matter of when we would be left to fend for ourselves in the massive, icy cold grey water that surrounded us.

As I peered over the rampart of the boat, I could see the rolling waves above the boat, and then the boat would be above the water. I could not see land in any direction. As far as I could see in every direction was water, rolling cresting waves of water. I was uncertain of our fate at that moment. Our guides were using a foreign language, but I could still understand the panic in their voices and the satanic expletives, that are universal to all languages.

Under duress of perishing from the earth, they cut all our gear loose, and out into the bay. It quickly disappeared in the waves. It felt as if our chances of surviving improved at that moment. Sadly, we were sure that we would never see any of our gear again.

The boat crews immediately started making their way to the shore. The boat scene was like the scene from the movie Leap Year.

When we made it to shore, we came across a fishing cabin on the beach area. We could see smoke and smell food. That was all the invite that we needed.

We quickly made friends with the occupants and volunteered to clean and organize the cabin in exchange for some of their fish and potatoes.

It felt so good to stuff our faces with those boiled potatoes and fish. I ate until my belly was satisfied. We were so busy not starving at that moment, that I am not sure if we left any food for them, either way they were kind enough to share their food with us.

They had a short-wave radio. And they had some form of a rudimentary runway. An arrangement was made between our leaders and these fishermen to secure air passage for us back to Churchill. A short while later an airplane, possibly a DC4 landed on the flat near the cabin.

It was a cargo plane. We sat on plywood benches among the freight and cargo that was being transported. At that moment we did not seem to care, our bellies were filled. We were not in a boat battling the waves. Most importantly we were headed to somewhere warm and dry.

A short while later we landed in Church Hill and secured train tickets, to take us back to near where we had left the trucks. We made it! We had begun our journey back home after having traversed some 450 to 500 miles in the subarctic wilderness and lived!

Later phone calls were made from pay phones along the route to arrange for our parents to collect us along the freeway interchange.

When I arrived, my parents looked at me with some disbelief. I was a little beat up and straggly looking and barefoot. It had become too painful to wear our shoes due to the trench foot.

Trench foot is the result of being wet and cold for an extended period. It is so named because the soldiers in WWI would get it as a result of being in the cold and wet trenches for extended periods.

Once home I had plenty of stories to tell my overly anxious parents. Who unbeknown to me had learned the fate of another group of 25 that had been in the same area. Apparently, but one of them had drowned. And now I knew the reason and source of the search and rescue helicopter.

Ocean currents are a funny thing. A few weeks after returning, we were notified that some of the canoes had washed ashore. Arrangements were made to ship them via train back home.

A short while later I received a photo of Carter with his Seal River Expedition canoe. Much of the green paint was gone and it was proudly wearing the dents and scars of the trip, flat bottom and all.

What I gained from this experience:
- I learned to improvise - to make do with what was in hand.
- Stories to tell.
- Independence – self-reliance.
- Sometimes persevering is the only way out or through a problem.
- Self-worth, comes from doing, achieving.
- That I can do hard things.
- An appreciation for that which we have.
- Increased survival skills.
- That people can change. Sometimes they just need a little nudge. A zero can become a hero.
- That success comes by sticking with it. Sometimes one step or one paddle at a time.
- A love of the outdoors, God's incredible creations and beauty.
- How individual actions help the group.
- I didn't just know it; these things were burnt into my mind in an indelible way. I had been educated by the grand master of teaching - experience.

Here are some points of interest about taking a Seal River trip that I located on the internet.

Duration: 21 days (I think we were out 27 days.) We returned after Labor Day in September

Difficulty Ratings River Travel: Advanced

Lake Travel: Advanced

Portaging: Difficult

Remoteness: Advanced

Technical Guide: Filled with class I to IV rapids, almost continuously

Special Comments: Do not attempt to paddle the Hudson Bay!

<u>Not for the faint-hearted or the amateur. Very remote, extremely challenging, continuous whitewater,</u> and even the possibility of polar bear encounter at the river exit into Hudson Bay.

12 PUT THE BAR BACK

For the sake of our youth, we must quit lowering the bar. It seems that when our sons are faced with adversity or challenges, the current popular technique is to lower the bar of expectation, to the point where our sons can just fall over it. Parents want to bulldoze every obstacle to lay a clear and level path for their child. We work countless hours and spend large amounts of money and energy to eliminate every challenge that presents itself in the path of our youth. As leaders we want to find every creative way possible to give them credit, even when it is not deserved. We want to check them off, as if the 'list' were the objective. We have forgotten that growth and the forge to strength of character lies in the struggle to achieve and overcome the obstacle by exerting oneself.

A recent example in the news is the debacle at Harvard of the affluent parents buying their son's or daughter's way into Harvard, instead of having them enter based on merit or achievement.

Yes, there is the fear that they may not be chosen or that someone may beat them out. This competition is good and drives improved performance. The individual is improved through the process of reaching and achieving. Remember, try then try again?

Interfering in such a manner defeats the very thing the parent is hoping to achieve. The interference stifles the child from developing and knowing the satisfaction of having earned it on their own. It weakens the character and one will quickly learn that to get ahead or to win, they too must cheat their way through life.

Competition is a desirable motivator and drives improvement. It is one of the ingredients in the recipe that makes this country great and exceptional.

By contrast making everything easy, may feel good for a moment. But it perpetrates a fraud and makes the achievement meaningless and diminishes self-esteem and the value of accomplishment.

Raise the bar, put it back where it belongs. Don't remove it, help them overcome it.

13 HEARTS AND THE WORD 'SERVICE'

One of the truths that I have discovered, is that is it not possible to know the joy and benefits of service until one becomes engaged in doing it.

Another truth that I discovered along the journey is that most young men want to be someone's hero.

During my time with Troop #210, the Scouts and I put together several service projects around our community. In no time, people were taking notice and they began to point us towards even more opportunities to help. Serving others brought us great joy.

As we cleaned, hauled, repaired, collected food, and provided services, I noticed changes in the boys. In the beginning the mention of "Let's go serve someone" would cause the Scouts to break eye contact and start making lists of all the things that they would rather be doing. That list would include most anything except service. Any attempt to coerce them or push them along would be met with resistance. It just sounded like something they didn't want to do until, they did it.

Because of this, I thought I needed to disguise the service projects for a while. As we were working, I noticed the smiles on their faces and the general good feeling that we were having while doing for others.

The Scouts were seeming to enjoy our projects. They related to me that they liked how they felt when they were giving of themselves. The Scouts were also enjoying learning life skills while engaged in these activities.

As a former landscaper, I taught them how to do basic lawn care, mend fences, and other skills to name a few.

When I asked, "How does learning to prune or to build a fence make you feel?" Some of the responses were "I felt that I was making a difference"

"I learned something that I could use"

"It feels good to do for people, especially the ones that can't do for themselves"

"I feel good inside."

I gathered from this that these boys do want to learn, they do want to make a difference, and they do want to be a part of something good. In a vacuum these natural desires get twisted or focused on other activities that are perhaps more entertaining and less productive. I affirm that they will by default turn to the time wasters or even destructive activities when they are not provided the opportunities to experience these ideals.

It is not enough for us to simply tell them. They respond best when we roll up our sleeves and get down in the trenches alongside them. They need men who will step up and show them the way. The reward; they quickly and readily follow – something that is moving. If you teach them that doing good is a cool thing, they will in turn pass it along.

The challenge to ourselves is to make sure that we are going in a desirable direction.

Service is something that I thought the boys would never ask to do, at least in the beginning. It is such a simple thing, and yet it has far reaching results. The whole world seems to turn a little easier as a result of helping and lifting others. When service is given, both the giver and the receiver are changed. Both are elevated and moods are lifted.

Expressing love to another being through giving of oneself changes and heals hearts. I can't think of a better way to make the world a better place than to give a hand up to our fellow beings.

There is peace and a sense of well-being when we are in the service of others. The Scouts can feel it and they know it is a good thing.

Could your communities' benefit from simple acts of service? Is there a better way to express that we care? Is there a better antidote for depression or selfishness?

The way the Scouts' behavior and their sense of well-being changed encouraged me. I knew that we were into something that was beneficial not only to the community but to Scouts themselves. They were becoming changed by the experiences.

As a testament of the impact of service in Scouting, I recently read a newspaper article that expresses the concern that we are going to feel the absence of the Eagles Scouts in the coming years. In Utah alone there were over 5000 Eagle Scout projects that were completed this past year!

As we go forward and with the Church of Jesus Christ withdrawing at the end of this year there will be tens of thousands fewer Scouts. There will be tens of thousands fewer Eagle and Scout service projects in the coming years, at least in our mountain west region.

Our communities, our nation, even our world, still need them, the Scouts and their service!

This is yet another reason in the long list of why the values of Scouting are worth fighting for.

Paul Fowler

My dad often repeated the words, "You can lead a horse to water, but you can't make him drink."

Many of those that I encounter along the way use similar words when it comes to working with the youth. I think we at times look for an excuse to fail because we really don't want to make the effort. So, we look for something else to blame it on. It is true that we cannot force anyone to partake of the water (programs) that we offer. But the statement itself is an incomplete thought. I believe it also implies that we must set the table in a manner that is appealing and inviting. The window dressings need to be in place. The water needs to be fresh and drinkable. Our programs need to be dynamic and meaningful, inviting and filled with substance.

I believe that our youth can spot a fraud. They recognize whether you are sincere in your actions with them or if you are just marking time. They want to see you do it first. Whatever you are serving, be the first one to try it.

If it is appetizing and they refuse, it's on them. Just be sure it is.
Paul Fowler (#PTFSM)

14 WHAT PEOPLE MISS
Scouts have changed the course of human history for the better, repeatedly. They'll do it again.

Some of you may be questioning some of my antics and methods. "What is this Scoutmaster thinking?" I am happy to share with you that I feel that Scouting needs to be dynamic, to hold the boy's attention, and pique their curiosity. My desire is for them to experience new things. They need to overcome their fears and build their self-esteem. Most importantly, self-worth comes not by taking the easy route, but rather through doing and accomplishing. This is a dynamic about boys becoming men that the world does not understand or acknowledge. They want to earn bragging rights. Hey, it was also fun!

In a world where many of the role models lack integrity, our sons need role models who truly possess it. One quick glimpse into the public figures portrayed by modern media is enough to make any one cringe. Do we really want our youth modeling them? Our country, our world and our communities, need men of integrity and character, now more than ever. Boys want heroes and, in a vacuum, they will find those heroes in less favorable places, like pro sports or other popular, but less scrupulous public figures.

In a world of me and only me, our sons need to see that there is a better way, that in truth it isn't all about me, it's about what I can do to make it better.

Many of the activities that our youth are involved in today promote selfishness and narcissism. Compare this with Scouting, which when properly applied, wrings the selfishness out of the boy and installs selflessness in its place. A Scout learns to do for others.

Imagine sometime later in the life of a young man who has performed dozens to hundreds of hours of service, who has walked countless miles in adverse conditions, ridden a bike for 50, slept in subzero weather, completed a mile swim, helped countless strangers in need, learned life and survival skills, conflict resolution, climbed mountains, fed the hungry, served his community, persisted in completing tasks, and has learned truly how to lead. Imagine if you will, a young man who has developed a knowledge of God and an appreciation for his creations and this beautiful earth, one who is a Patriot, one who knows how to do hard things. A young man who has been set on a path of service to others, love of God and country, and of course service to himself, by taking care of his own physical and emotional well-being. Now, imagine him facing off with life's challenges. He will be a force for the greater good and there will be nothing that he can't accomplish, no hill that he can't climb.

With these skills learned early in life, his trajectory will be set. Success in life will be his for the taking. This is how Scouting changes lives. There is nothing else that prepares them, for success in this manner. Many of the other activities available to our youth, are time wasters or hinderances to success. Scouting activities while designed to be fun are far more than mere entertainment.

Of all the activities from your youth, which are the ones that you would place on a resume? Which one provides the best value?

Google famous Scouts or look up what Eagles have done. So, few of them, yet they have done so much. It will amaze you.

Duty to God

**A Scoutmaster's role is to lead them to know God.
From the Scout oath, the first obligation is to God.**

Paul Fowler

15 THINGS I WISH PARENTS UNDERSTOOD

We live in a time of fascinating technology. Yet, with all its wonderment, inventors and leaders in the tech world don't give the tech that they invent to their own children. What do they know that we miss?

They know that these electronic gizmos are not intended for young minds. They are aware of the detrimental effects of these devices of convenience. I am of course referring to smart phones and iPads and the untethered access to the world of the internet.

If your son has unsupervised access to the internet, he already knows more about the birds and the bees, than you will ever know or want to. This exposure is our fault, it rests upon us to train them, supervise them and yes limit the use of these devices. They require limits, supervision and training in the same manner as does driving a car or using a firearm.

Cell phones have the potential for great good and for incredible evil and harm. There are apps designed to be secretive and hide information from you. There are apps and people that are encouraging our sons to do unspeakable things, including how to be evasive and to play with your mind as a parent.

Electronics are like eating a mental diet of glazed donuts. They make our kids lazy, mentally, emotionally, and spiritually. Their use stimulates depressing thoughts and they encourage anti-social behaviors. If you ever see an anxious and disengaged kid at Scout camp, he will be the one with the cell phone. The phones cause them to think more about what they may be missing back home instead of focusing on what they could be doing at camp. They are a needless source of stress and anxiety.

In the words of one of my colleagues, a cell phone is equivalent to a "pet rattlesnake." Yet, too many of us give our kids a cellphone, without training or supervision, because we don't want to make the effort to invest our time in them. This is unfortunate because what they need most is some of our time. My life experience tells me that it isn't even that important how that time is spent so much as we spend the time with them. They get a sense of how important they are to us by the amount of time that we invest in them. They will forever be grateful for the time and remember it the most.

Scouting is much more than just another activity. It is leadership development disguised as a game. It is being surrounded by people that are encouraging you to go and do good. It is reinforcing moral and family values. It is learning by doing and becoming a good citizen. It by design aides us to be mentally, physically, and spiritually fit. Scouting is teaching youth to make moral and ethical decisions throughout their lifetimes. This is achieved through using methods that have been proven for more than 100 years. The activities, the hikes, the camping, the service projects, starting fires with no matches, the challenging adventures, and the privations, are all things we use to build and develop the youth. These activities are designed to teach and to expose youth to real life experiences. It is not merely another activity from the list to choose from.

It takes four to five years for the values to become ingrained into your son. It cannot be rushed and there are no shortcuts. When parents rush it, using the check list method, they rob their son of the deeper more meaningful growth opportunities. While Scouting done in this manner may allow your son to receive the badge, it will not produce the lasting, life changing results that we are hoping for.

To attempt to rush the results is much like picking sweet corn before its time. Corn cannot be picked according to the calendar or by a certain date. It must be fully ripened on the stalk to achieve the juicy sweetness before harvesting. It will not ripen or continue to grow off the stock, it will only rot. No one wants to eat a partially developed ear of corn. It will then be discarded. Scouting, like sweet corn, that is rushed will result in harvesting before fully developing or ripening and the values will too soon be forgotten or discarded. The result is that it will have little effect on the life of the boy.

We sometimes give your son difficult challenges to overcome. Our activities will sometimes stress your son. Encourage them, but don't do it for them. It is an intended element of the program. It is not all designed to be easy.

The fun times will hold their attention in the short run. The challenging ones will change them and the course of their lives for the long run. Encourage them and support them to see it through.

A Scoutmaster who accepts slipshod work and parents who push for it set a standard that slipshod or lackadaisical efforts will be accepted throughout his life. This creates the opportunity for that individual to be extremely disappointed at a later date. It is far better to hold them to true standards and expectations now. Their lives will be ever more successful and happier from having had the experiences. Parents are often guilty of accepting half-baked efforts in their competitive mind sets to have their sons complete the checklist and advance. We are doing our youth a disservice when we promote the path of least resistance.

We further defeat the system and deny our sons the opportunity for growth and leadership development when we focus on advancement or checklists. At other times, we as parents, protect them to the point of holding them back. We are afraid that they could get hurt or fail so we don't allow them to try. <u>We fail to see that it is the experiences that provide the catalyst for change and growth. It is the struggles that teach the greatest and most lasting lessons.</u>

Kids, especially teens will always be curious. They are hard-wired to learn by seeking information and to emulate what they see. This is a natural and wholesome desire. This is a great advantage when used correctly. Like water though, youth tend to seek information from the path of least resistance.

Getting them outside and into nature and hiking is like eating a diet of broccoli, salads, and every other nutritious food that they need to consume. Hiking is a mood enhancer and it is an antiserum for heart disease and depression. It has been proven true that people who spend time in the outdoors in nature live happier and healthier lives. They have an increased positive outlook, something that we all could benefit from.

Too many organized sports kill the imagination; conversely, being out of doors and in nature enhances it. Sadly, in today's world sports are used to overbook our sons. They are no longer the simple neighborhood contests that they once were. Besides, in Scouting all the youth can have equal playing time. The only bench sitters are the ones who choose to sit out.

Despite the hype, many other activities are not teaching our youth anything regarding integrity or a work ethic, or mental toughness, or leadership, or even life skills. In fact, they often teach that the world revolves around them and that others need to cater to them. They help create an oversized sense of self-importance.

The result of attempting to make everyone 'feel good' by eliminating obstacles and challenges is that the current generation seems to want everything provided for them. They lack an appreciation of what it means to earn something. We have created the entitled society and it is growing worse every day. The mentality of providing every need and fighting every battle for them is proving to be detrimental.

Moms, it is emotionally and mentally healthy for your sons to spend some time away from you and you need time away from them. They need to learn to do for themselves. And the time away helps to prepare you both for the future.

One of the greatest gifts I ever received from my dad was being taught how to work and the idea that we all need to contribute. These time-proven ideas are in opposition to the world that teaches our youth to take all that they can get. Scouting, much like the old family farm, teaches personal accountability in a world that wishes to teach them to never take personal responsibility.

I have found with my own kids, Scouts, and even my grandkids, that they learn best when we roll up our sleeves and work alongside them. It just goes smoother when we are the example of what we are asking them to do or to be. Youth seem to learn behavior by imitating what they observe. This is why getting out and getting involved is so powerful and effective.

16 CONCLUSION

My life has been full of 'do overs'; my wife reminds me that if I would get it right the first time, I wouldn't need them. She loves to quickly remind me that I need practice to get things right. I guess do overs will continue to be a recurrent theme for me.

Within Scouting, I felt that I had found a place to 'make a difference'. A place to give back to others and to society. And much like the Scouts, I wasn't willing to quit on something that I had invested in. I had spent a great deal of time and effort getting into Scouting, acquiring equipment, and developing skills to work with our youth. During this time Scouting had taken its effects on me as well. I too now have the words "Do a Good Turn Daily" written in my subconscious. As I walk through life the words of the Scout Oath and Law echo in my mind. A Scout is Trustworthy, Loyal, Helpful, Friendly, Courteous, Kind, Obedient, Cheerful, Thrifty, Brave, Clean and Reverent. And the Oath, On My Honor, I will Do My Best to my Duty to God and my Country, and to obey the Scout law, to help other people at all times, to keep myself physically strong, mentally awake, and morally straight. These words affect and influence the choices that I make. How different the world would be if more people truly lived these words.

My wife and I experienced some life changes that included selling our home. It also meant giving up my role as Scoutmaster in Troop #210. We moved to a new city.

I had invested heavily into Scouting and decided to give it another shot by volunteering, this time around. I had served several times now, as one that had been voluntold, or obligated if you will. I was now becoming passionate about Scouting. I subsequently went into our local Scout troop and I volunteered to serve.

It was a religious unit, and the look on the Bishop's face was priceless. Volunteered? Who volunteers for this?

A short while later Bishop Perry, asked us to come back over for a visit and at that time invited us to be the leaders of the 11-year-old Scouts in Troop #436. This is where Cael, Chris and Jackson entered my life and my role as a leader of 11-year-old Scouts, began all over again. I was given a 'do over', a chance to be better than I was before. This time, I sought to Do MY Best! And now, I was not only armed with more experience, and needed mentors, I had a purpose and I was becoming passionate in my desire to help our youth.

From my earlier experiences, I knew that they want to be doing, they want to be a part of something that is happening, something that is moving. Just like in sports, everyone wants to be a part of the champion team. We and they find it desirable to be associated with successful groups.

These young men love to learn and to be shown new things. If we don't direct them and lead them along on the correct paths, they will spend their desire and energy going into less favorable paths and following anything else that moves. It is in their nature to do so. As guardians of the rising generation, it is our responsibility, our obligation, even our opportunity to recognize this and to provide adventurous character-building experiences for all youth.

Leaders teach by doing. Boys learn by seeing. Many of us want to lecture them, instead of showing them. So much more can be learned in a week of practical exercise versus months in a classroom. Learning is enhanced by physical involvement.

Through experience I observed that the boys cannot learn if the adults dominate the activity. The Scouts will quickly lose interest if the adults don't give way and allow the boys to engage. I see this in many programs followed by the words, "No one wants to participate."

It is true that it is painful, at times, to allow them to fumble through some of the activities and leadership opportunities. Could we do it better? Most likely. But then we fail in our objective to raise boys and build leaders.

I had the great advantage of growing up on a family farm where I learned to be moving and to get stuff done. Our parents made it such that you were motivated to be engaged in a productive cause.

My dad would turn me loose on a project and then get out of the way. He somehow had the patience to watch me fail or mess up. He had the wherewithal to make sure I got back up on my own, sometimes under duress. But he made sure that I got back up. He taught me that failure is a necessary and powerful teacher.

He also made sure that we understood that quitting was never an option. We could change directions or methods, but quitting was never an option.

We had gardens to weed, animals to feed, and crops to plow. Everyone had to contribute to get it all done. We worked together as families and as a community we came together to help each other. We learned that each of us had a role to play.

Dad taught us to feed the animals before we fed ourselves and we had to have our chores complete before we ever came to the table. Though, I did not always appreciate his methods as a kid, I love that my father taught me the value of hard work.

A turn back towards the values of the family farm life would be a blessing on our society today. Whether we know it or not, we are missing the lessons and the values that were inherently taught growing up in rural America.

By comparison many of our youth today lack a work ethic and are very self-centered. Parents seem to be too concerned with their child being comfortable to the point that it hinders their ability to teach them. We need to assist them with a paradigm shift from "What can I get?" to "What can I give?"

Our youth still need the lessons of work, community, helping, being physically active and contributing to the greater good. All of these values, which were once part of daily rural life in America, can still be found in the Scouting movement.

Sometimes the ability to get stuff done is referred to as a work ethic. Whatever it is called I was in possession of it. And yet to truly be an effective Scout leader, I needed refinement. My earlier Scouting adventures, including my trip to Canada as a youth gave me experiences. Even so, I was not prepared to work with the youth. This came only after a period of earnestly seeking skills and knowledge. Refinement, like a good wine, comes with time.

The effectiveness of the types of experiences offered through Scouting is life changing. It is truly tragic that we do not always value these life and leadership lessons. Scouting is so much more than mere entertainment. It offers opportunity for personal improvement, association with adults of character, leadership, and exposure to the Scouting ideals. Where else can they learn outdoor, survival and emergency skills? Additionally, Scouts learn to work with others to accomplish goals, and they develop a sense of community.

When compared to other activities that your son could be involved in, nothing compares in the breath and scope in making a difference in the trajectory of their life. Scouting is well rounded in its ability to teach life skills; to improve academics, conflict resolution, work ethic, and family; and ultimately succeed in life.

These positive, time-proven values are needed now, more than ever. We need men and women of Honor, Integrity, and Valor. We are desperately in need of people who know how to lift and to build. Our society needs problem solvers, and people who step up and do the right thing, well, simply because it's the right thing to do. That's why I believe the values of Scouting are still worth fighting for! I hope this book will encourage you and others to see the value and influence that we can have.

I hope that you will be encouraged to pass our values on to the coming generation and to be a guide to them.

I hope that you see that we too, can help change the future by investing in our youth and helping them to soar to new and stretching heights.

This generation is our opportunity and our responsibility. I hope that you will go and make a difference!

I hope that you will become passionate.

Paul Fowler

APPENDIX
Notebooks

Somewhere along the way I began to make notebooks of our journeys. I recorded some of the impressions that I was receiving about working with these young men. I felt pulled or lead along by a loving and guiding Heavenly Father to work with these Scouts, these young sons of God. He was teaching me, giving me the knowledge that I needed to develop my skills and attitude in working with these Scouts. I found it to be easy and I became self-motivated once I gained a purpose and a vision of building boys to men. HE was telling me that they mattered.

Here are some samples of those impressions that I felt.

- "Be moving. You can't follow something unless it is moving!"
- "Scouts need a way for each Scout to record his own story along the journey."
- "It is not about what you would do, it is about what you have done. Now go and build on what you have begun and do more!"
- "We are preparing them to face future challenges that the world will throw up against them."
- "Their character values will be learned from you."
- "If it isn't stretching you, it isn't influencing you."

Paul Fowler

INSPIRE THEM TO LEAD

Thoughts and more thought. As time passed, I was learning to write them down as soon as I had them. Procrastination was a punishing thing, when it came time for recall.

- Instead of telling them what to do, show them.
- Create opportunities for them to lead.
- Teach them in brief moments, 30 seconds to 3 minutes max. Keep it short.
- Lead out, go and do. Teach them to get up and do.
- Boys need men to teach them to be men, manly men.
- Young men need shepherds. Be the kind that God expects.
- Show them that they CAN.
- Be yourself, they need your experience. Don't hide your heritage, use it. (Growing up on family farm).
- Pull the Scouts along to higher standards.
- They don't like to be pushed. They want to be shown, and then they want to do it for themselves.
- Get out of the way.
- Let them fail and teach them to pick themselves up.

Paul Fowler

LITTLE PHILMONT

I was always seeking knowledge and skills that I could use with the Scouts. I sought ways to improve my abilities and the overall experience for the youth. I felt that the program needed to be more dynamic. It needed to be somewhat fluid to adapt to the varying personalities of the boys. It also needed both some consistency and a certain level of surprise to hold their attention. It needed a why or purpose.

I searched for anything that might help me teach and lead these Scouts. I knew that I needed help. And I needed to find my stride. To realize that part of being a Scoutmaster is just being myself. To learn to use the vast experiences of my own life to lead and influence these young men.

Little Philmont produced by Trapper Trails Council became one of those moments of change for me. I met up with fellow Scouters, and leaders. We shared experiences and insights. We had some fun and we attended our classes like good Scouts would do.

I loved the experience of camping with fellow Scouters and enjoying a crackling fire and a meal together. It felt good to know that we are not alone in our roles as shepherds of the rising generation.

At least three of the presenters left a remarkable impression on me. The first one, spoke of making efforts to wear the full Scout Uniform. Another presenter spoke of the aims and methods of Scouting. The third was a loss prevention specialist.

This event took place at the Bartlett Scout reserve in Montpelier, Idaho. It was one of those rainy weekends that did not disappoint in its ability to produce mud. And the mud on this weekend was spectacular! It was a sticky, track it up on your shoes and clothes, kind of mud.

In the pouring rain, we hiked to the fire bowl on the Redman side. The presenter, Elder Laing, stood there in a very expensive looking suit, white shirt, tie and of course some Italian leather shoes.

He related to us how he was asked to wear his uniform when he accepted his current position as a General Authority of the Church of Jesus Christ. He further explained that his uniform was a suit and tie. He explained, their meaning and purpose, how they change behavior and expectations, how they help us identify with a group.

The part that made the connection with me, was when he said, "If I can stand here in this weather, wearing my uniform, you can wear yours", meaning our Scout uniforms. He was modeling the behavior that he desired in each of us.

That was the moment that my uniform became a part of me, of expressing who I am. This overpriced set of activity clothing that I was wearing now had a purpose and meaning. His image standing there in the rain and mud, in his uniform, is still vivid in my memory. I have never failed to wear mine from that time.

Several of the courses presented at the event, spoke to us about what seemed to be an endless list of rules and a list of all the things that you can't do.

I was feeling very limited and beginning to understand why many of the troop programs that I had witnessed were so watered down and boring. I thought I was seeing why it was that they lacked luster and challenge.

As I attended the next speaker, he seemed to be reading my mind. As I walked into his session he began with these words.

"Many of you are probably thinking that we don't want you to do anything fun. That you are restricted from doing anything exciting or adventurous."

He had my attention as he continued.

"I want to assure you that that is not the case. We want you to have programs that are dynamic and challenging. We just want to help you mitigate loss and injury. We understand that these types of activities come with a certain level of risk."

I left that presentation feeling less restricted and knowing that it was permissible to bring exciting and challenging activities into our program. In fact, it was expected to have dynamics to create interest that will draw the boys in and hold their attention. Shooting, climbing, water sports and other activities were all open and available for us to use. I found this refreshing and it amped up my enthusiasm for the program.

I now understood that the watered -down version was more a product of the leaders or their own lack of understanding than the program itself.

I gained a motivation to seek out additional training in these areas so that we could build dynamic challenges and activities into our youth program. This became something that fed my own enthusiasm for Scouting as in the process I met and became friends with other enthused and skilled Scouters.

The third presenter challenged us to learn the eight methods of Scouting. I memorized them along with the Aims of Scouting that weekend.

Once I had committed them to memory, my approach became more balanced. I recognized the imbalance of the program due to the over emphasizing of only one or two of the eight methods. In fact, much of my misconception of Scouting was due to the culture of advancement only, that was so prevalent in many of the troops in our area. There was no emphasis on experiences or character and leadership development. They were not only missing the methods, but they were not implementing the Scouting ideals. Many had no idea why they were even participating in Scouting. Their attitudes seemed to be based upon being obligated, rather than passionate, in their participation in working with the youth. They lacked purpose in their approach.

As the weekend progressed, I was becoming more animated in my desire to contribute and to be a Scoutmaster. By the conclusion of the weekend, I understood that at least part of my earlier misconception of Scouting was derived from the lack luster and slipshod implementation of it. I was excited to know that in its heart, the more dynamic program still existed. It just needed some old school salty personalities to be involved.

ABOUT THE AUTHOR

Paul Fowler   #PTFSM

Paul is an Entrepreneur. He has more than four decades of business and leadership experience. During which time, he has built several successful companies.

As Scoutmaster he is a recipient of the Scoutmaster Key, Unit Award of Merit, District Award of Merit and Silver Beaver. He is a member of the Order of the Arrow, an NRA Training Counselor and Shooting Sports Instructor.

He serves as a member of the Trapper Trails Shooting Sports Committee. He has also served as staff for shooting sports at the Council and National Levels, including National Camp School for the BSA.

Paul is happily married to his wife Pam. They have five children and sixteen grandchildren.

Paul was raised on a farm in the Midwest, were he learned the value of thrift and work. He has a passion for working with youth. As a Scout he survived, a near month long, expedition canoeing and porting over 450 miles, in the sub artic region of Manitoba, through the Seal River system and into the Hudson Bay, eventually ending in Church Hill, Manitoba.

FB @paul fowler
Instagram PTFSM
https://bsatroop126.org/blog-ptfsm

Amazon.com/Paul Fowler

Please, if you enjoyed this book, take a moment and write a review!

www.ingramcontent.com/pod-product-compliance
Lightning Source LLC
Chambersburg PA
CBHW031451040426
42444CB00007B/1056